WITHDRAWN

*graphic designers
in the USA/1*

graphic designers

in the USA/1

Louis Danziger
Herb Lubalin
Peter Max
Henry Wolf

Universe Books ✴ *New York*

Edited by Henri Hillebrand
English texts by the artists
Design by Gan Hosoya

Published in the United States of America
in 1971 by Universe Books
381 Park Avenue South
New York, N.Y. 10016

Copyright 1971 by Bijutsu Shuppan-sha, Tokyo
and Office du Livre, Fribourg

Library of Congress Catalog Card
Number: 76-147895
ISBN 0-87663-141-3
Printed and bound in Japan

Table des matières   *Table of contents*   Inhaltsverzeichnis

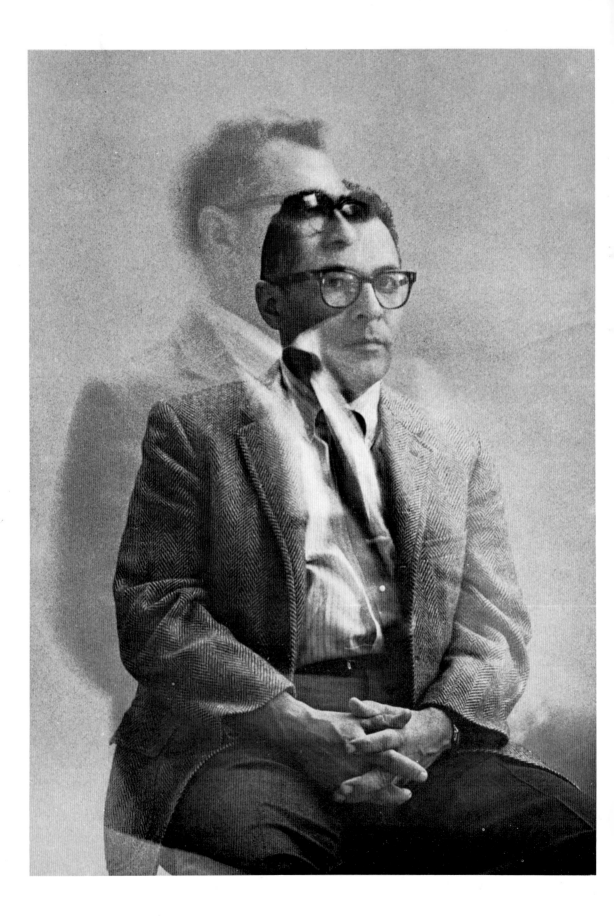

Louis Danziger

Pour nous graphistes, le problème de la création est essentiellement différent de celui de l'artiste dont l'œuvre ne subit aucune contrainte commerciale. En effet, notre travail, destiné à un public très large, est soumis, d'une part aux exigences de ce public, d'autre part à celles très spécifiques de nos clients. Notre œuvre est fonction de trois critères d'appréciation absolument différents, sans être nécessairement antagonistes: la satisfaction du client, du public et de nous-même.

Nous devons, si nous acceptons une commande et voulons répondre aux exigences de nos clients, user non seulement de talent, mais aussi d'intelligence. Socialement responsables, nous essayons d'obéir à ces impératifs d'une manière positive. Nous tentons d'offrir une information juste, un divertissement et un plaisir esthétique.

La plupart des graphistes seront, je pense, d'accord avec moi sur ce qui précède. C'est plutôt sur le plan de la satisfaction personnelle que les objectifs et les méthodes de travail diffèrent.

Les postulats de base qui m'aident à trouver cette satisfaction et me

The problem of the graphic designer is quite different from that of the artist who deals essentially in the private image. Because of the public nature of our work and because our commissions are generally problems of a specific nature, we find that we are continually trying to satisfy the needs of three distinctly different but not necessarily antagonistic criteria. The three are the client, the audience, and one's self.

We must, if we accept a commission, use our skill and judgment to achieve our clients' objectives. As socially responsible people we try to accomplish these objectives in a positive way. We do this by performing some service for our audience. We provide information, entertainment, and aesthetic pleasure.

Most designers will, I believe, agree with the above. It is in the area of self-satisfaction where the methods and goals of designers vary. The concerns and approaches that provide satisfactions for me and direct the nature of my work are as follows:

I am concerned with finding an image that is visually strong and

Uns Graphikern stellt sich das Problem des künstlerischen Schaffens wesentlich anders dar als dem Künstler, dessen Werk keinerlei kommerziellen Zwängen unterworfen ist. In der Tat muß unsere Arbeit, die für ein sehr breites Publikum bestimmt ist, sowohl den Ansprüchen eben dieses Publikums als auch den sehr spezifischen Forderungen unserer Kunden genügen. Unser Schaffen ist drei ganz und gar verschiedener Kriterien unterworfen, die einander dennoch nicht unbedingt widersprechen müssen: der Zustimmung des Kunden, der des Publikums und nicht zuletzt unserer eigenen Zustimmung. Wenn wir einen Auftrag annehmen und den Forderungen unserer Kunden entsprechen wollen, müssen wir nicht nur von unserem Talent, sondern auch von unserer Intelligenz Gebrauch machen. Unsere gesellschaftliche Verantwortung verpflichtet uns, nach Möglichkeit diesen Forderungen im positiven Sinne zu genügen. Wir versuchen, die wahrheitsgemäße Information, die wir liefern, mit Unterhaltung und ästhetischem Genuß zu verbinden.

Louis Danziger

guident dans mon travail sont les suivants:

Je recherche une image qui soit visuellement puissante et dont la forme esthétique adhère si pertinemment à l'idée qu'il devient difficile de séparer la forme de l'idée.

On éprouve un sentiment d'aboutissement lorsqu'on parvient à résoudre un problème graphique d'une manière élégante, («élégant» considéré ici dans le sens scientifique: expression maximale d'une idée par un minimum de moyens).

Dans mon travail, j'essaie de me laisser guider par mon intelligence intuitive. Il y a en moi continuellement une aspiration à la clarté et à la profondeur, plutôt qu'à l'intelligence rationnelle.

Et, bien qu'obligé de reconnaître que le travail que nous faisons soit, par son aspect pratique, éphémère, produire une œuvre qui sorte de l'ordinaire et qui semble toujours neuve est une source de grande satisfaction, même après vingt ans et plus.

Le rythme de travail imposé par le volume toujours croissant de la demande incite un nombre toujours plus grand de graphistes, parmi les plus qualifiés, à s'occuper de la direction et de l'administration de la publicité plutôt qu'à son exécution effective.

aesthetically gratifying yet so pertinent to the idea that it becomes difficult to separate form from content.

There is a sense of achievement when one can solve a design problem in an elegant way. (The word "elegant" is used here in the scientific sense: the accomplishment of a great deal with a minimum of means.)

I am concerned with the production of work that demonstrates intelligence. There is continually a search for clarity and depth rather than cleverness.

Although I recognize that the work we do is essentially ephemeral, it is a source of satisfaction to produce work that avoids faddishness and looks fresh over a period of twenty years or more.

The pressures imposed by the volume of work and the sheer magnitude of the clients move most successful designers more and more into the areas of direction and administration and away from the actual execution of work. For myself, I prefer to do less work and continue to remain more directly involved in its production. This involvement extends into photography. With but few exceptions, all of the photographs seen in my work are produced by myself. Designing is a source of much satisfaction and many frustrations,

Vermutlich werden die meisten Graphiker über das bisher Gesagte mit mir einig sein. Was aber die persönliche Befriedigung betrifft, so sind unsere Ziele und Arbeitsmethoden sehr verschieden. Die Grundprinzipien, die es mir ermöglichen, künstlerische Befriedigung zu finden, und mich in meiner Arbeit leiten, sind folgende: Ich versuche eine wirkungsvolle Bildvorstellung zu entwickeln, deren ästhetische Form sich mit der Idee so eng verbindet, daß sich eines vom andern schwerlich mehr trennen läßt.

Man hat das befriedigende Gefühl, wirklich etwas erreicht zu haben, wenn es einem gelungen ist, ein graphisches Problem auf elegante — und das heißt: ökonomische — Weise zu lösen. (Der maximale Ausdruck einer Idee, realisiert mit einem Minimum an Mitteln.)

In meiner Arbeit strebe ich vor allem nach Klarheit und Gediegenheit und versuche, mich darum mehr von meiner Intuition als von rationaler Intelligenz leiten zu lassen. Und obwohl ich zugeben muß, daß unsere Arbeiten infolge ihres zweckbedingten Charakters nur kurzlebig sein können, bereitet es mir außerordentliche Befriedigung, ein Werk zu vollbringen, das sich vom Üblichen unterscheidet und selbst noch nach zwanzig oder mehr Jahren neuartig wirkt.

Das von der Vielzahl der Aufträge diktierte Arbeitstempo bringt es mit sich, daß sich im Werbefach eine immer größere Anzahl der besten Graphiker statt mit kreativen Aufgaben mit der Leitung und Administration der Geschäfte befassen muß.

Was mich betrifft, so ziehe ich es vor, weniger Arbeiten zu übernehmen, um mich dafür mehr und intensiver mit den Problemen der Gestaltung auseinandersetzen zu können. Dasselbe gilt auch für die Photographie. Mit wenigen Ausnahmen habe ich die Photos, die in meinen Arbeiten Verwendung fanden, selbst aufgenommen.

Louis Danziger

Quant à moi, je préfère restreindre mon travail et rester plus directement concerné par les problèmes de production. Cette motivation s'étend également à la photographie. A part quelques exceptions, j'ai réalisé toutes les photographies figurant dans mes travaux.

La publicité est une source, à la fois de grandes satisfactions et de bien des déceptions, mais j'ai toujours pensé qu'elle donnait, d'une façon originale, le sentiment d'être utile et qu'elle apportait un immense enrichissement.

but I have always felt that it makes one useful and very special—and that of course provides the greatest satisfaction.

Das Werbefach kann dem Graphiker künstlerische Erfüllung bieten — aber auch viele Enttäuschungen bereiten. Mir jedenfalls hat es noch stets ' und auf unvergleichliche Weise das Gefühl gegeben, nützlich zu sein, und damit eine unermeßliche Bereicherung bedeutet.

1923	Né à New York.
1938-1941	Etudie les arts plastiques au collège et dans les «Federal Art Project Classes».
1938	Fait un stage dans une imprimerie pendant ses vacances scolaires.
1939	Fait un stage pendant ses vacances scolaires dans une maison d'impression en sérigraphie.
1940-1941	Fait des dessins de scène pour des compagnies en tournée d'été.
1942	Assistant du directeur artistique du «Delehanty Institute», New York.
1942-1945	Effectue son service dans l'armée américaine.
1946	Assistant du directeur artistique de la «War Assets Administration», Los Angeles.
1947	Stage de perfectionnement avec Alvin Lustig.

1923	*Born in New York City.*
1938-41	*Studied a variety of arts in high school and in Federal Art Project classes.*
1938	*Apprentice at printing firm during school vacation.*
1939	*Apprentice at silk-screen printers during vacation.*
1940-41	*Stage designer for summer repertory companies.*
1942	*Assistant to the art director, Delehanty Institute, New York.*
1942-45	*Military service.*
1946	*Assistant art director, U.S. War Assets Administration, Los Angeles.*
1947	*Studied with Alvin Lustig.*
1948	*Designer at "Esquire" magazine, New York. Studied and worked with Alexey Brodovitch, New York.*
1949	*Began design and consultation practice, Los Angeles.*

1923	In New York geboren.
1938-1941	Studium der angewandten und freien Kunst in Abendschulen und in «Federal Art Project Classes».
1938	Arbeitete während der Schulferien als Lehrling in einer Druckerei.
1939	Arbeitete während der Schulferien als Lehrling in einer Siebdruckerei.
1940-1941	Bühnenbildner für diverse Theaterensembles auf Sommergastspielen.
1942	Assistent des Art Director am «Delehanty Institute» in New York.
1942-1945	Militärdienst in der amerikanischen Armee.
1946	Assistent des Chefgraphikers der «War Assets Administration» in Los Angeles.
1947	Fortbildungskurs bei Alvin Lustig.

9

Louis Danziger

1948 Créateur pour le magazine «Esquire», New York. Travaille avec Alexey Brodovitch, New York.
1949 S'installe comme créateur et conseiller esthétique à Los Angeles.
1950 Appelé comme professeur à l'«Art Center School».
1955 Expose seul à «STA», («Society of Typographic Arts»), Chicago.
1957 Voyage d'un an en Europe.
1964 Nommé professeur à la «Chouinard Art School».
1965 Voyage plusieurs mois au Japon.

Nombreuses distinctions dans le domaine de l'Art graphique, décernées par les «Art Directors Club» et «A.I.G.A.».
Travaux publiés dans toutes les revues et livres concernant l'art graphique aussi bien aux Etats-Unis qu'à l'étranger.
Travaux présentés dans les expositions des «Art Directors Club», «Museum of Modern Art», New York, «Museum of Art», Los Angeles, et à la «Library of Congress».

1955 One-man show at STA (Society of Typographic Arts), Chicago.
1957 One year of travel in Europe.
1965 Travel in Japan.

Taught advertising design for several years at the Art Center School, and since 1964 at the Chouinard Art School (now the California Institute of the Arts), Los Angeles. Has served on juries at the New York and Los Angeles Art Directors Shows, the AIGA Printing for Commerce Exhibition, the STA show, and other exhibitions. His works have been represented internationally in many books and periodicals on graphic design and have been exhibited in every major advertising design exhibition in the United States and several abroad. Has received medals, certificates, and other awards. Works are in the collections of the Museum of Modern Art, New York, the Los Angeles County Museum of Art, and the Library of Congress.

1948 Gestalter bei der Zeitschrift «Esquire» in New York. Arbeitete zusammen mit Alexey Brodovitch, New York.
1949 Selbständiger «Graphic Designer» und Formgestalter in Los Angeles.
1950 Berufung als Lehrer an die «Art Center School».
1955 Einzelausstellung, veranstaltet von der «Society of Typographic Artists» (STA), Chicago.
1957 Ganzjährige Europareise.
1964 Ernennung zum Professor an der «Chouinard Art School».
1965 Reise nach Japan, mehrmonatiger Aufenthalt in Japan.

Zahlreiche Auszeichnungen auf dem Gebiet der graphischen Kunst durch den «Art Directors Club» und das «A.I.G.A.».
Arbeiten erschienen in allen graphischen Fachzeitschriften und ungezählten Büchern sowohl in den USA als auch im Ausland.
Arbeiten wurden in Ausstellungen des «Art Directors Club», des «Museum of Modern Art» in New York, des «Los Angeles Museum of Art» und in der «Library of Congress» gezeigt.

Louis Danziger

Louis Danziger

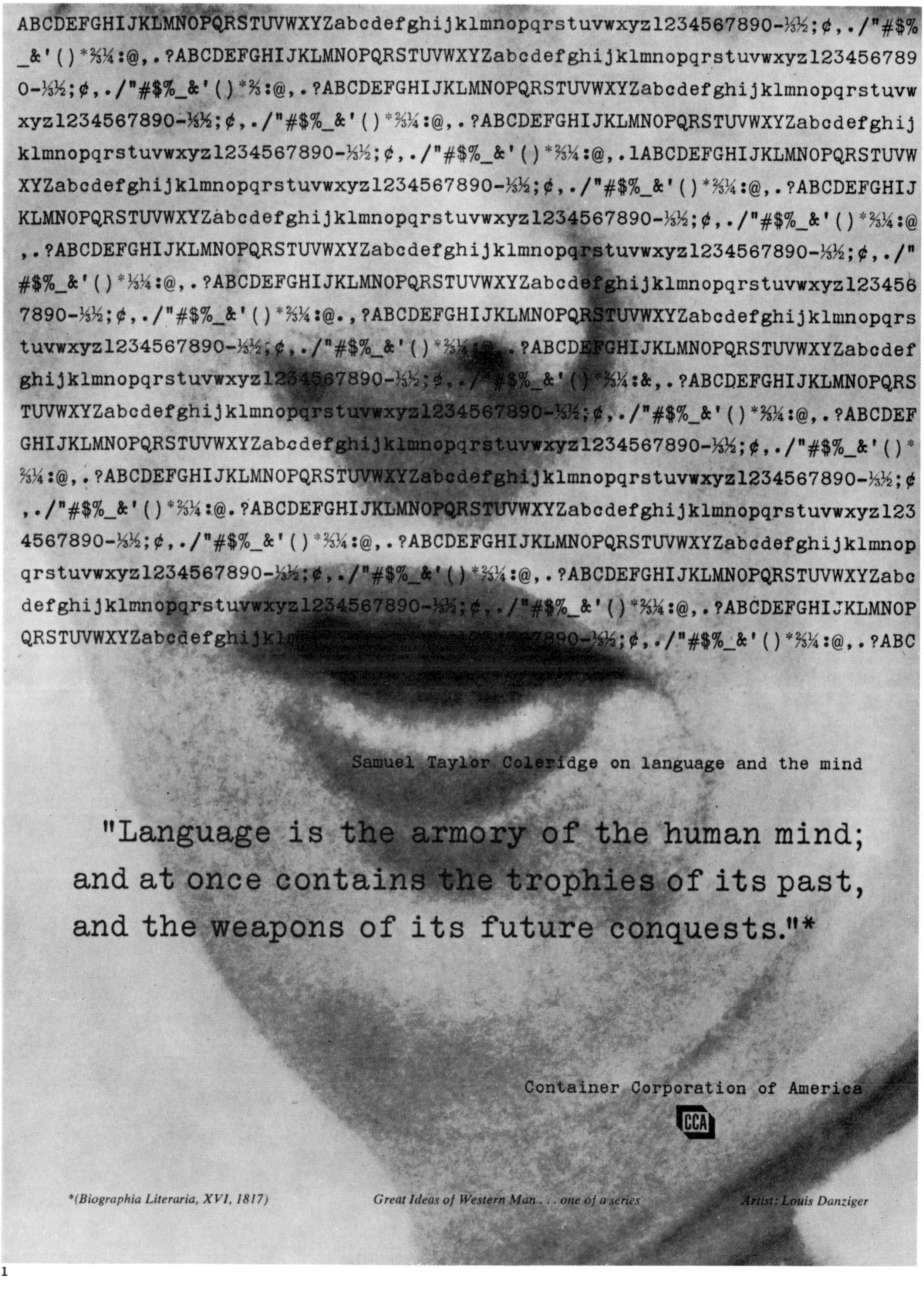
ABCDEFGHIJKLMNOPQRSTUVWXYZabcdefghijklmnopqrstuvwxyz1234567890-⅓½;¢,./"#$%
_&'()*⅔¼:@,.?ABCDEFGHIJKLMNOPQRSTUVWXYZabcdefghijklmnopqrstuvwxyz123456789
0-⅓½;¢,./"#$%_&'()*⅔:@,.?ABCDEFGHIJKLMNOPQRSTUVWXYZabcdefghijklmnopqrstuvw
xyz1234567890-⅓½;¢,./"#$%_&'()*⅔¼:@,.?ABCDEFGHIJKLMNOPQRSTUVWXYZabcdefghij
klmnopqrstuvwxyz1234567890-⅓½;¢,./"#$%_&'()*⅔¼:@,.1ABCDEFGHIJKLMNOPQRSTUVW
XYZabcdefghijklmnopqrstuvwxyz1234567890-⅓½;¢,./"#$%_&'()*⅔¼:@,.?ABCDEFGHIJ
KLMNOPQRSTUVWXYZabcdefghijklmnopqrstuvwxyz1234567890-⅓½;¢,./"#$%_&'()*⅔¼:@
,.?ABCDEFGHIJKLMNOPQRSTUVWXYZabcdefghijklmnopqrstuvwxyz1234567890-⅓½;¢,./"
#$%_&'()*⅓¼:@,.?ABCDEFGHIJKLMNOPQRSTUVWXYZabcdefghijklmnopqrstuvwxyz123456
7890-⅓½;¢,./"#$%_&'()*⅔¼:@.,?ABCDEFGHIJKLMNOPQRSTUVWXYZabcdefghijklmnopqrs
tuvwxyz1234567890-⅓½;¢,./"#$%_&'()*⅔¼:@,.?ABCDEFGHIJKLMNOPQRSTUVWXYZabcdef
ghijklmnopqrstuvwxyz1234567890-⅓½;¢,./"#$%_&'()*⅔¼:&,.?ABCDEFGHIJKLMNOPQRS
TUVWXYZabcdefghijklmnopqrstuvwxyz1234567890-⅓½;¢,./"#$%_&'()*⅔¼:@,.?ABCDEF
GHIJKLMNOPQRSTUVWXYZabcdefghijklmnopqrstuvwxyz1234567890-⅓½;¢,./"#$%_&'()*
⅔¼:@,.?ABCDEFGHIJKLMNOPQRSTUVWXYZabcdefghijklmnopqrstuvwxyz1234567890-⅓½;¢
,./"#$%_&'()*⅔¼:@.?ABCDEFGHIJKLMNOPQRSTUVWXYZabcdefghijklmnopqrstuvwxyz123
4567890-⅓½;¢,./"#$%_&'()*⅔¼:@,.?ABCDEFGHIJKLMNOPQRSTUVWXYZabcdefghijklmnop
qrstuvwxyz1234567890-⅓½;¢,./"#$%_&'()*⅔¼:@,.?ABCDEFGHIJKLMNOPQRSTUVWXYZabc
defghijklmnopqrstuvwxyz1234567890-⅓½;¢,./"#$%_&'()*⅔¼:@,.?ABCDEFGHIJKLMNOP
QRSTUVWXYZabcdefghijkl
890-⅓½;¢,./"#$%_&'()*⅔¼:@,.?ABC
Samuel Taylor Coleridge on language and the mind
"Language is the armory of the human mind; and at once contains the trophies of its past, and the weapons of its future conquests."*
Container Corporation of America
CCA
*(Biographia Literaria, XVI, 1817)
Great Ideas of Western Man . . . one of a series
Artist: Louis Danziger

1

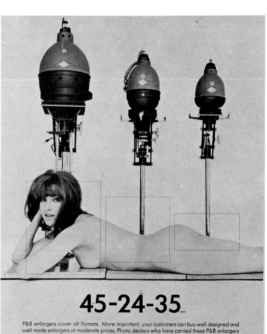

kobena super 8 for the creative film maker

7

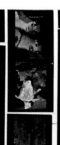

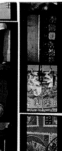

mamiya/sekor

500TL
f2.0

mamiya/sekor

Mamiya Camera Company, Ltd., Tokyo, Japan

8

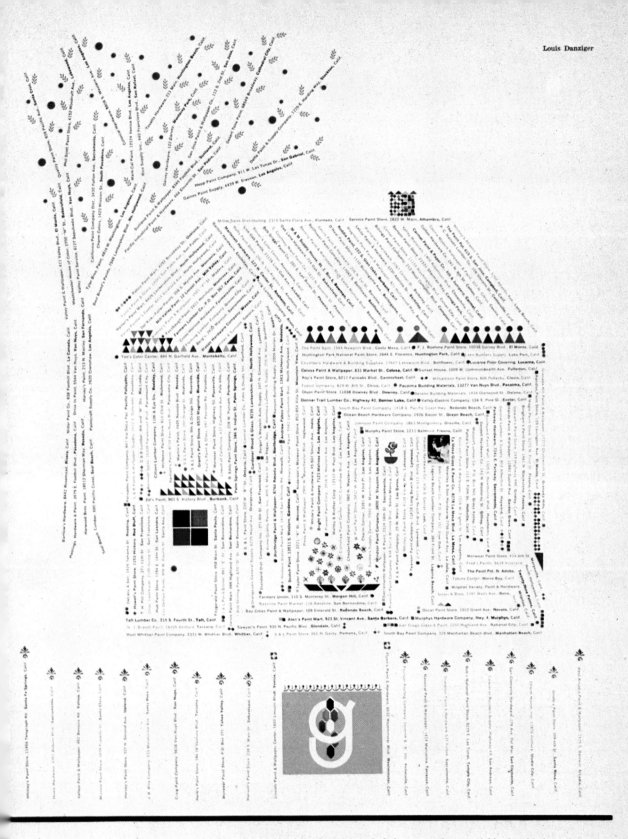

10

11

31 Yakushi Nyorai
Early Heian period, ninth century
Wood (Height) c. [...]
Gangō-ji, Nara
Registered National Treasure

The healing Buddha, Yakushi Nyorai (Sanskrit: Bhaiṣajyaguru) made twelve vows to heal the physical and mental ills of all sentient beings. He generally holds a medicine jar in his left hand and raises his right arm, bent at the elbow, with the palm of the hand turned out. Worship of Yakushi began in Japan a little later than that of [...]

12

32 Kannon Bosatsu
Asuka period, seventh century
Gilt bronze (Height: 30¾")
Hōryū-ji, Nara
Registered Important Cultural Property

[text columns]

33 Nyorai
Asuka period, seventh century
Gilt bronze (Height: 14½")
Vairocana Daibutsu-ji, Ōita
Registered Important Cultural Property

[text columns]

13

35 Zaō Gongen
Heian period, eleventh century
Wood, polychromed (Height: 36")
Kinpu-ji, Nara
Registered Important Cultural Property

[text columns]

THE IMITATION REAL THING ¶ The first warning alerted posts all over the United States and Canada. Unidentified airborne objects seemed to be approaching at supersonic speeds from many directions. ¶ Simultaneously in control centers throughout North America men and machines dealt with torrents of data. Watching blips on radar scopes, crews made decisions which ordered weapons to destroy the attackers. Interceptor pilots reported over loudspeakers. As the enemy reacted and shifted, fresh instructions crackled through command phones. ¶ But no rockets were fired. No bombs fell. The blips came from magnetic tapes made by a single high-speed computer. Called Operation Desk Top, this was a simulated raid—the most gigantic ever arranged—to exercise the North American Air Defense System. In planning it, SDC made four billion calculations and six and one-third miles of magnetic tape. ¶ To train managers in decision-making, to exercise decision-makers under realistic stress, to avoid costly errors in actual operations—these are some of the purposes of SDC's pioneering work in systems research and development. **SYSTEM DEVELOPMENT CORPORATION.** A non-profit scientific organization developing large-scale computer-based command and control systems. Staff openings at Lodi, N. J. and Santa Monica, Calif.

DOES YOUR PACKAGE SING?

PHOTOGRAPHER: LOUIS DANZIGER

Ours most certainly do.
So well they stir the consumer's chemistry of choice.
How do we give this power to your package?
By artfully blending exclusive market research findings
with color, typography, texture and surprise
into compelling pretested designs
that accelerate the sale.
It is our business to design packaging
that speeds your marketing cycle
from the point of production
to the decisive moment of purchase.

CONTAINER CORPORATION OF AMERICA

16

17

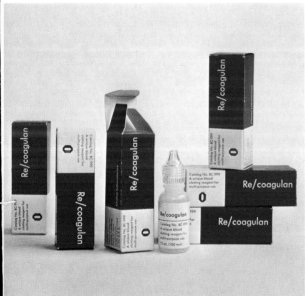

18

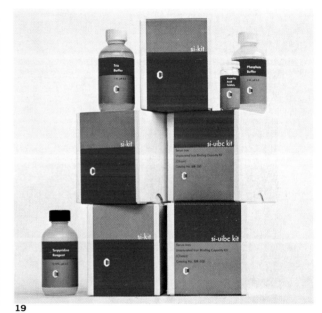

19

20

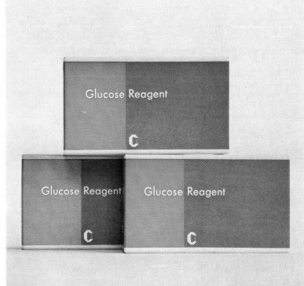

21

To protect the rights of barbers, it is illegal for a surgeon to shave you in the city of London. Barbers, however, under Henry VIII were allowed to continue with minor surgery and dentistry. In fact, they were hacking away at patients in France and Germany for years after it was forbidden in England. The surgical-barber shop of those days was a scene of incredible chaos. The shop was a refuge for idlers and the clearing house for news and gossip. Waiting customers were entertained by lute or viol players. Amid this tumult, beards were shaved, teeth were pulled, and men were bled. It is easy for laymen to laugh at barber-surgeons and lute players in the operating rooms. But those of us in the general field of medicine know the obstacles that were overcome along the road to modern medical practice. Progress was painstaking, built on the contributions of dedicated men. We take pride in this development. And at Clinton Laboratories we are justly proud of the modest contributions we have made through Hemotrol and Chemtrol. These are natural, internal standard controls. They go through each step of the procedure in parallel with the patient's blood, insuring maximum accuracy. Hemotrol is a stable blood, which serves to standardize any hemoglobin procedure. Chemtrol, on the other hand, is a freeze-dried serum. It is used to control 19 different clinical chemistry determinations, from glucose through transaminase, including protein-bound iodine, albumin, and the globulins.

Complete technical data available on request.

Products of progress from CLINTON LABORATORIES

6010 Wilshire Boulevard, Los Angeles 36, California

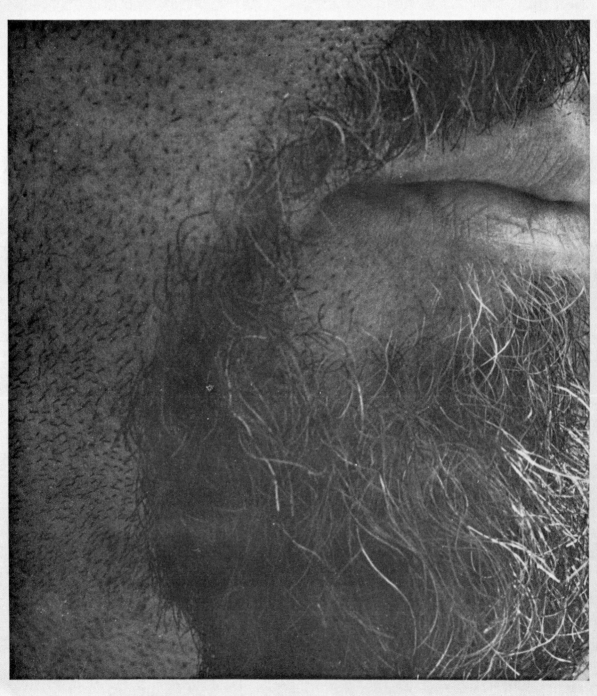

"Wait! I see my mother again. She's singing her lullaby now. 'Hushaby, my baby...'" A young clergyman with a brain injury is the subject of an experiment. A wire with a weak electrical current is applied to his brain. He sees his mother so clearly it is as though she is standing in front of him. His eye, however, is not seeing. His brain is remembering. By creating an artificial visual image the surgeon was able to pinpoint a specific brain center. One small dot on the map of brain function that science pieced together—bit by bit. This devotion to the aims of science—call it the search for truth—has made possible most of our insights to man's makeup. And, it gives us a good feeling to know that in our way at Clinton Laboratories we are adding to the tools of science. One of our products, Chemtrol, is used to control 19 different clinical chemistry determinations. From sugar through transaminase, protein-bound iodine, albumin and the globulins. Chemtrol is a natural, freeze-dried serum. As an internal standard control it goes through each step of the procedure in parallel with the patient's blood, which insures the highest possible degree of accuracy.

Complete technical data available on request.

Products of vision from CLINTON LABORATORIES

6010 Wilshire Boulevard, Los Angeles 36, California

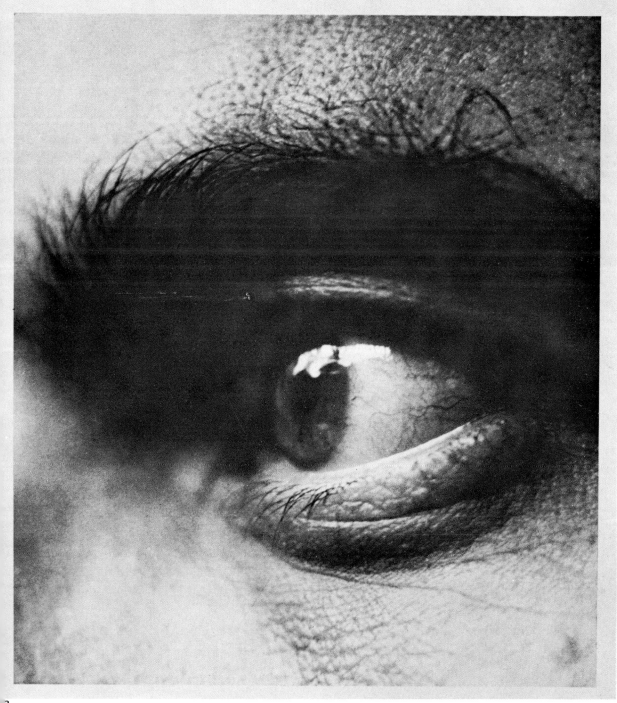

3

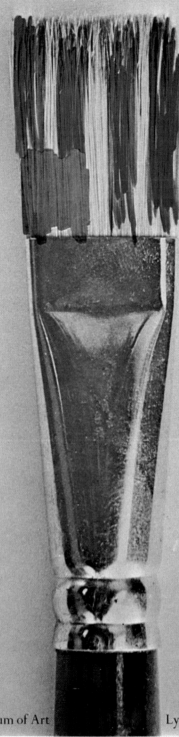

Los Angeles County Museum of Art   Lytton Gallery   June 3 - July 31, 1966

CROSSROADS

What are the directions of the arts?

This is the provocative theme
of the 5th International
Design Conference.
From June 13th to 18th in
Aspen, Colorado, distinguished
thinkers from all parts of the
world will gather to explore
design in its broadest sense.
For complete details and list of
speakers write to:
International Design Conference
220 South Michigan Avenue
Chicago 4, Illinois

DESIGN: LOUIS DANZIGER

25

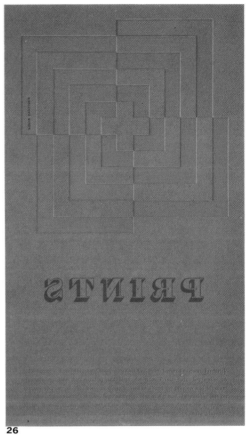

26

27

28

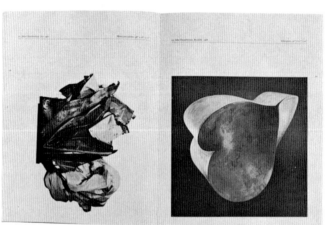

29

30

31

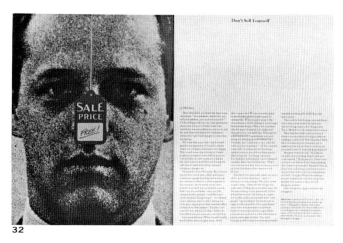

32

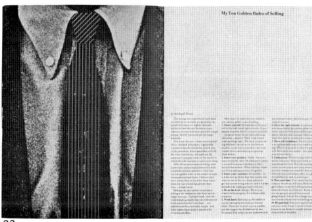

33

34

35

Designed by Louis Danziger

Eye-catching aluminum foil printed by Koltun Bros., Lithographers, 418 N. Fairfax Avenue, WEbster 3-8433

"The play," Hamlet observed saltily, "was caviare to the general." Too precious to waste on the hoi polloi, caviar has long been *the* gastronomic symbol of wealth, even nobility. Nutritious (70% more protein than egg yolk), expensive (1 oz. beluga costs $2), caviar is even supposed to be a powerful aphrodisiac (Catherine the Great fed it to her lovers). Whatever its heritage and mythology, caviar remains, for the gourmet, a delight to the palate. Unfortunately, for the sufferer from hyperthyroidism, it can be a pain in the neck. Who can afford to *buy* caviar can be determined only by one's banker. Who can afford to *eat* it must be determined by one's physician. And for this determination, physicians depend on the medical laboratory. Aware that reliability is vital to the laboratory's contribution, Clinton Laboratories provide diagnostic tools as dependable, as precise, as mod-

ern technology can make them. One, Chemtrol, is a serum with known values for standardization and control of 30 blood chemistry determinations. Tested in parallel with the unknown specimen, Chemtrol is a continuous check on accuracy and reproducibility of a method, on improper technique, on deterioration or faulty reagents, on operation of equipment. Without Chemtrol, such determinations can be a tough roe to hoe.

Complete technical data and sample on request.

Products for diagnosis from CLINTON LABORATORIES

6010 Wilshire Boulevard., Los Angeles 36, California.

38

The bonbon got its name from the French—it means good-good, high praise indeed from a people who pride themselves as gourmets. Modern sophisticated Americans bring boxes of candy to favored friends. Sweets to the sweet, so to speak. Or to put it another way, candy is dandy—except, of course, for a diabetic. Which is where the laboratory comes in. The physician relies on the laboratory findings when diabetes is suspected. Just as he relies on them for many of his diagnoses. At Clinton Laboratories we are aware of the vital role of the laboratory. Our products reflect this need for reliability, as in our Glucose Reagent. Glucose Reagent is a specific enzymatic test for the simple and rapid determination of glucose in blood and urine. The entire test is conducted in one cuvette, and no deproteinization, heating, or filtering is required. Pretty sweet, huh?

Complete technical data and sample available on request

Products of reliability from **CLINTON LABORATORIES**

6010 Wilshire Boulevard, Los Angeles 36, California

31

Your great-grandmother thought there was magic in salt. She did more than season food with it—she threw it over her shoulder for luck; she was positive she could catch a bird by salting its tail. In her world salt was a wonderful thing to have—and still is. But to a man with a specific heart or kidney disease, salt can mean possible death. The physician depends upon the medical laboratory for much of his diagnostic information—to find out "who can have salt." We acknowledge this growing importance of the laboratory. By improving our products constantly we are keeping pace with the demands made upon laboratories. Take Hemotrol, for example. Unlike the Cyanmethemoglobin standard, Hemotrol serves as a standard throughout the entire hemoglobin determination. It is a stable blood. A natural, internal standard control, Hemotrol goes through each step of the procedure in parallel with the patient's blood, insuring maximum accuracy. This is the way we earn our salt.

Complete technical data and sample available on request.

Products for diagnosis from CLINTON LABORATORIES

6010 Wilshire Boulevard, Los Angeles 36, California

"Now there is a new, improved **Chemtrol** from Clinton Laboratories. This standard control serum for blood chemistries now has known values for 22 constituents. More than 20 qualified laboratories participate in the analysis of each lot. **Chemtrol** is now available in a convenient package of four 5 ml. vials. Contact your dealer or Clinton Laboratories, 6010 Wilshire Boulevard, Los Angeles 36. Tell him a little bird told you so."

41

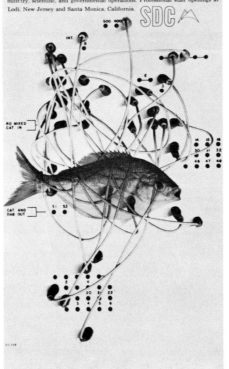

America's fast-changing defense system is steadily improving and strengthening as new weapons and control systems are fitted in. But each change in defense procedure must be tested under stress. How and where can this be done without disrupting the existing system? Some new kind of simulated test zone is needed.

the simulated sea   System Development Corporation has worked out the intricate answer around Kansas City. On computers and magnetic tape, it has simulated tricky features of many defense zones: a seacoast in mid-Kansas, an imaginary island at Denver, a Canadian border in Iowa. In this Model Operational Environment, as it is called, crews and computers react to hypothetical attacks as radar data (live, simulated, or a mix) comes in. Thus continental defense reaches ever-higher levels of preparedness. SYSTEM DEVELOPMENT CORPORATION A non-profit corporation developing large computer-based control systems for military, scientific, and governmental operations. Professional staff openings at Lodi, New Jersey and Santa Monica, California.

42

How do you make correct decisions in controlling our defense forces, in directing air traffic, in managing a network of distant factories? Modern society increasingly relies on vast information processing systems, composed of men and machines, to help make these decisions. ¶ To study man-machine systems, we are building a new kind of general purpose simulation facility: Systems Simulation Research Laboratory. Its central element will be a very large digital computer. The laboratory will be used to: search for principles for allocating tasks to men and machines; devise improved languages for man-machine communication; develop methods of modeling and simulating large, intricate organizations. ¶ Our objective is to develop a body of basic knowledge about principles that affect the design of these systems. **SYSTEM DEVELOPMENT CORPORATION.** A non-profit scientific organization developing large-scale computer-based command and control systems. Staff openings at Lodi, New Jersey and Santa Monica, California.

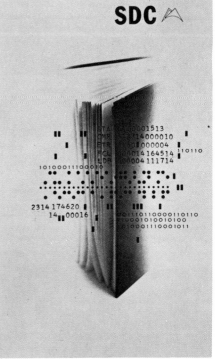

43

44

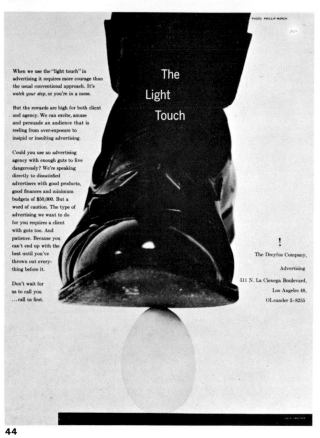

PHOTO PHILLIP MARCH

The Light Touch

When we use the "light touch" in advertising it requires more courage than the usual conventional approach. It's *watch your step*, or you're in a mess.

But the rewards are high for both client and agency. We can excite, amuse and persuade an audience that is reeling from over-exposure to insipid or insulting advertising.

Could you use an advertising agency with enough guts to live dangerously? We're speaking directly to dissatisfied advertisers with good products, good finances and minimum budgets of $50,000. But a word of caution. The type of advertising we want to do for you requires a client with guts too. And patience. Because you can't end up with the best until you've thrown out everything before it.

Don't wait for us to call you ...call us first.

!

The Dreyfus Company, Advertising

511 N. La Cienega Boulevard, Los Angeles 48, OLeander 5-8255

45

40

PETROLEUM WORLD

DECEMBER 1950
fifty cents a copy

46

Hard Sell vs Soft Shell

If you're an advertiser, try this simple test. Record your own reactions to the average advertising message.
Does it make you mad, un-sell you on what might be an intrinsically fine product? Then you've discovered that too often hard sell does the *opposite* of what it's supposed to do. You can't smash your egg and eat it too!
Now look at your own advertising. Is it dramatic enough to capture the attention of a consumer exposed to over 200 advertising impressions *each* day? Does it add excitement and desire to your product, or does it use a sledgehammer to open an egg?
Are we getting to you? Well if you're a dissatisfied advertiser with a good product, good finances and a minimum budget of $50,000, let's get a little closer.
As an advertising agency we never write ads to a captive audience. We aim for the fugitive audience. That demands tremendous imagination and the guts to stick by a new idea even when the client's glance is a little chilly. The results speak for themselves, both in ads and client sales. And we'd love to show the proof. Call us. We won't bore you with platitudes and self-praise but present a sensible plan that will give you a chance to test our claims at a nominal cost, and without obligation. Write or call us now, while we're young and eager, and before great success permits us to raise our minimum to $250,000.

!

The Dreyfus Company   511 N. LaCienega Boulevard, Los Angeles 48. Oleander 5-8255

47

How long should an extension cord be?

Long enough to reach all your branch plants, offices and warehouses, no matter how big your organization, so that sales statistics, inventory reports, engineering data and other key facts and figures of your business flow into your data processing center fast enough to go on time to the people who must act on them. If this isn't happening now, one of the reasons may be that your data processing center is here, and your branches are out there.

There's a way around it, of course. Collins Data Communications. A Collins Kinetape magnetic tape or Kinecard punched card transmission system can dramatically extend the use of your data processing center, linking it to all branch or regional locations via existing telephone or other common carrier communications lines.

The cost of installing a Collins Kineplex® Data Communications system can be far less than the cost of duplicating and staffing computers. And with Kinetape or Kinecard, which transmit data twice as fast as any other current commercial equipment, you'll be taking a giant step toward maximum use of your existing data processing system.

We'd be happy to tell you more about building or improving data networks with Collins Data Communications systems. Please write to **Collins Radio Company**, Western Division, 2704 W. Olive Avenue, Burbank, California.

COLLINS

Collins Radio Company, Burbank, California/Cedar Rapids, Iowa/Dallas, Texas

The First Generation

William Baziotes	Hans Hofmann	Richard Pousette-Dart
Willem De Kooning	Franz Kline	Ad Reinhardt
Arshile Gorky	Robert Motherwell	Mark Rothko
Adolph Gottlieb	Barnett Newman	Clyfford Still
Philip Guston	Jackson Pollock	Bradley Walker Tomlin

Los Angeles County Museum of Art, Lytton Gallery. June 18 through August 1, 1965

Museum Hours: 10-5 Tuesday through Sunday. Closed Monday

Special Hours: The New York School Exhibition will be open Tuesday evenings from 5 until 10 p.m.

Admission Fee: Adults $1.00—Children through 18 years 25¢. Catalogue available

New York School

Herb Lubalin

De nos jours, s'il veut réussir, le graphiste ou le directeur artistique doit saisir toutes les phases de la communication. Il doit comprendre qu'il participe à l'effort total de communication, qui commence avec un client évolué, espérons-le, continue avec une idée qui donnera forme et personnalité au produit que l'on veut lancer, et aboutit au porte-monnaie du consommateur. Entre deux, il y a le graphiste et le directeur artistique, l'expert en esthétique d'emballage, le point de vente et l'équipe de promotion, plus une douzaine d'autres personnes.

Les «experts en communication», qui devraient avoir une connaissance approfondie et le respect de la contribution de chacun, ne parviennent tout simplement pas à communiquer entre eux.

Se perfectionner dans tous les domaines de la communication, tel est le mot d'ordre qui explique le succès de notre firme. Nous savons qu'un emballage rationnellement conçu est un apport publicitaire de poids; une réclame stimulante peut inciter le consommateur à entrer dans un magasin, mais son effet

To succeed today, a graphic designer or art director must understand the melding of all phases of communications. He is a part of a total communications effort that starts, we hope, with a progressive client, an effective corporate image, and a knowledgeable product designer and ends in a consumer reaching into his pocket for money to buy that product. In between are the advertising copywriter, the art director, a packaging expert, point-of-sale and promotional people, and a dozen others.

The problem has been that each person involved in the total communications effort thinks that his own thing is the key to marketing and selling that product. The "experts" within the communications pool just don't understand each other, and this causes a breakdown of communications between individuals who should not only have a thorough knowledge of each other's function but a respect for each other's contribution.

Our success is due to the fact that we have made it our business to become knowledgeable in every area of communications. We know

Ein Graphiker oder Art Director, der heute Erfolg haben will, muß alle Phasen der Kommunikation beherrschen. Er muß begreifen, daß er an einem Prozeß totaler Kommunikation teilnimmt, der — das wollen wir doch hoffen — mit einem fortschrittlichen Kunden beginnt, sich in der Idee, die dem auf den Markt zu bringenden Produkt Form und Gestalt gibt, fortsetzt und bei der Brieftasche des Konsumenten endet. Zwischen diesen beiden Polen agieren der Texter und der Art Director, der Verpackungs-Experte, die Leute von der Verkaufs- und der Promotionsabteilung sowie ein Dutzend weiterer Instanzen.

Die « Kommunikationsexperten », die ja über profunde Kenntnisse verfügen und die Leistung jedes einzelnen anerkennen sollten, sind offenbar außerstande, miteinander zu kommunizieren.

Die Lösung, der wir den Erfolg unserer Firma verdanken, lautet: Vervollkommnung auf allen Gebieten der Kommunikation. Wir wissen, daß sinnvoll konzipierte Verpackungen eine wesentliche Verkaufshilfe darstellen. Eine sti-

sera réduit à néant par un emballage peu fonctionnel. Inversement, un emballage bien pensé peut soutenir une publicité défaillante. L'époque du travail en vase clos est révolue.

C'est pourquoi la firme Herb Lubalin, Inc., est devenue Lubalin, Smith, Carnase, Inc. Notre clientèle requiert une idée et une image graphiques qui puissent être facilement assimilées à n'importe quelle forme de communication moderne. Nous devons donc nous exprimer aussi bien typographiquement que picturalement, nous devons créer pour la télévision, pour l'emballage et user de tous les procédés d'impression à notre disposition. Nous avons formé une équipe qui est à son aise dans tous les domaines de la communication. C'est pour cette raison, je pense, que notre compagnie est unique en son genre. Nous sommes spécialistes en tout. Nous prédisons que dans dix ans toutes les phases de la communication, aujourd'hui réparties entre différents spécialistes, point de vente, étalage, emballage, esthétique du produit, conditionnement, graphisme architectural, etc., seront confiées globalement à des équipes publicitaires comme la nôtre, travaillant indépendamment ou sous contrat, et la fusion de leurs connaissances en chaque matière permettra une exploitation

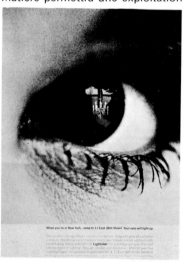

When you're in New York, come to 1 East 36th Street. Your eyes will light up.

how important a good package design can be to the creators of effective advertising. If a stimulating ad gets a customer into a supermarket, a poorly designed package can quickly kill the sale no matter what the ad accomplished. And, conversely, a great package can make advertising look good. The day of specialists working in their vacuums is over.

And this is the reason why Herb Lubalin, Inc., is now Lubalin, Smith, Carnase, Inc. As clients demand that images and ideas flow easily through all froms of today's communications, we must make it happen typographically and pictorially on the TV screen, in the package, and in all print media. We have brought together a team that can function in any one—or all—areas of communication. For this reason, I believe, our company is a one-of-a-kind organization—we are specialists in everything.

We predict that in ten years total communications teams within advertising agencies or retained by advertising agencies will take over all the functions—point of sale, display, packaging, product design, corporate design, architectural graphics, etc.—that were once farmed out to specialists and use their highly sophisticated methods to produce a much more effective marketing job for their customers.

I have been doing a good deal of thinking about youth lately—youth in our business and youth as a consumer. I have reluctantly come to the conclusion that young designers today are so interested in the getting rich quickly that they are not getting the background in all phases of communications and marketing, something that our field demands.

On the other hand, youth represents a gigantic buying public. Young adults comprise 35% of our population. We have to design for people 25 years old and under to sell. These young people are sharp, better educated than any

mulierende Werbung kann den Konsumenten veranlassen, ein Geschäft zu betreten, aber ihre Wirkung ist gleich null, wenn die Verpackung unzweckmäßig ist. Andererseits kann eine gut durchdachte Verpackung eine verfehlte Werbung weitgehend ausgleichen. Die Zeiten der «Scheuklappen-Arbeit» sind vorbei.

Dies ist der Grund, weshalb aus Herb Lubalin, Inc. Lubalin, Smith, Carnase, Inc. geworden ist. Unsere Kunden verlangen eine Idee und eine graphische Präsentation, die mühelos jeder Form moderner Kommunikation angepaßt werden können. Wir müssen uns deshalb ebensogut typographisch wie bildnerisch ausdrücken können. Wir arbeiten für das Fernsehen, für die Verpackungsindustrie, und müssen alle uns zur Verfügung stehenden Druckverfahren anwenden. Wir bilden ein Team, dem jedes Gebiet der Kommunikation vertraut ist. Dies ist, so meine ich, der Grund, weshalb unsere Firma in ihrer Art einzig dasteht. Wir sind Spezialisten in allem. Wir sagen voraus, daß sämtliche Phasen der Kommunikation, die heute noch auf einzelnen Experten anvertraute Spezialgebiete wie Verkauf, Auslage, Verpackung, Ästhetik des Erzeugnisses, Beschaffenheit des Erzeugnisses, architektonische Graphik usw. verteilt sind, in 10 Jahren ausnahmlos Werbeteams, die wie wir unabhängig oder unter Kontrakt arbeiten, überlassen sein werden. Die Verschmelzung der Kenntnisse auf allen Gebieten wird es ermöglichen, viel umfassendere Lösungen für die von unseren Kunden gestellten Probleme zu finden.

In letzter Zeit habe ich viel über die Jugend nachgedacht, sowohl über die in unserem Fach tätige, als auch über die konsumierende Jugend. Ich bin widerstrebend zu dem Schluß gelangt, daß unsere jungen Graphiker von dem Wunsch, rasch zu Geld zu kommen, so sehr besessen sind, daß es ihnen nicht

Herb Lubalin

plus complète des problèmes posés par nos clients.

Ces derniers temps, j'ai beaucoup pensé à la jeunesse, la jeunesse dans notre métier et celle qui consomme, j'en suis arrivé, bien malgré moi, à la conclusion que nos jeunes graphistes sont tellement préoccupés par le désir de faire rapidement fortune qu'ils n'ont plus l'esprit disponible pour saisir les subtilités du processus de la communication, ce qui est pourtant essentiel dans notre profession.

D'autre part, la jeunesse constitue un immense potentiel de consommateurs. Les jeunes adultes représentent 35 % de la population. Nous devons donc créer pour un public de 25 ans ou moins si nous voulons vendre. Ces jeunes ont l'esprit critique et sont plus instruits qu'aucune génération précédente. Ils ont bouleversé les lois traditionnelles de vente. Voyez simplement l'évolution de la mode masculine, de l'industrie automobile, des loisirs, ces deux dernières années! Le graphiste, lui aussi, doit être conscient de ces changements et sa création doit répondre aux exigences actuelles. Nous ne pouvons pas nous appuyer sur des principes statiques qui nous limitent à un type unique d'expression. Nous sommes parties d'un monde en mouvement. Récemment, j'ai accepté la présidence de l'«International Academy of Communicating Arts & Sciences». Le but unique de cette organisation nouvelle est d'établir la communication entre les différents «communicateurs». Nous espérons réunir des professionnels de toutes sortes, afin qu'ils puissent discuter, s'enrichir et se comprendre mutuellement. Les «communicateurs» d'aujourd'hui monologuent alors qu'ils devraient dialoguer. Il n'y a plus place, actuellement, pour une perspective étroite de la création graphique; le graphisme est intégré au monde toujours plus vaste de la communication, et c'est dans ce monde que nous travaillons tous.

other generation in the history of man. They are changing all the rules for successful selling. Look what's happened in the last several years to men's clothing, in the automotive industry, and in the entertainment industry because of youth. Designers, too, must understand the changes that are taking place in society today and be able to respond creatively to them. We cannot settle for one font of wisdom just as we can't settle for one font of type.

We must be creatures of the changing times. Recently I accepted the presidency of the International Academy of Communicating Arts and Sciences. This new organization's sole purpose is to bridge a gap—communicators are not communicating to each other. We hope to bring together men from all areas of the field so they can talk to each other, learn from each other, and most of all understand each other. Communicators today are talking to themselves, holding monologues, when they should be holding dialogues.
There is little room today for a narrow perspective on graphic design. In fact, design has been swallowed up by communications, and that's the world we are all working in today.

mehr möglich ist, die subtilen Nuancen des Kommunikationsprozesses zu erspüren, was doch in unserem Beruf von allergrößter Bedeutung ist.

Andererseits stellt die Jugend ein immenses Potential an Konsumenten dar. Die jungen Erwachsenen machen 35 % der Bevölkerung aus. Wenn wir uns verkaufen wollen, müssen wir uns deshalb auf ein Publikum einstellen, dessen Durchschnittsalter maximal 25 Jahre beträgt. Diese jungen Leute sind außerordentlich kritisch und viel gebildeter als jede frühere Generation. Sie haben die überlieferten Verkaufsprinzipien außer Kraft gesetzt. Betrachten wir beispielsweise die Entwicklung der Herrenmode, der Automobil- und der Vergnügungsindustrie in den letzten zwei Jahren. Auch der Graphiker muß sich dieser Veränderungen bewußt sein, und seine Arbeit muß den heutigen Forderungen entsprechen. Wir können uns nicht auf statische Grundsätze stützen, die uns auf eine einzige Ausdrucksart beschränken.

Wir sind Zellen einer in Bewegung geratenen Welt. Vor kurzem habe ich das Amt des Präsidenten der «International Academy of Communicating Arts & Sciences» angenommen. Einziges Ziel dieser neuen Organisation ist es, eine Verbindung zwischen den verschiedenen «Kommunikations-Spezialisten» herzustellen. Wir hoffen, die Fachleute aller Gebiete zusammenzubringen, damit sie miteinander diskutieren, Erfahrungen austauschen und einander besser verstehen lernen können. Die «Kommunikations-Experten» von heute führen Selbstgespräche, wo Dialoge nottäten. Die Zeit, da man die kreative Graphik nach engstirnigen fachlichen Gesichtspunkten beurteilte, ist endgültig vorüber. Die Graphik ist ein Teil der sich ständig erweiternden Welt der Kommunikation geworden, und es ist diese Welt, in der wir alle arbeiten.

Herb Lubalin

1918	Né à New York.	*1918*	*Born in New York City.*	1918	In New York geboren.

1918 Né à New York.
1939 Gradué de la «Cooper Union School of Art and Architecture».
1945 Nommé vice-président de la «Sudler & Hennessey, Inc.», directeur de la création et directeur de la section graphique «SH & L».
1964 Président de la firme «Herb Lubalin, Inc.».
1968 Fonde la société «Lubalin, Smith, Carnase, Inc.» avec Ernie Smith, Tom Carnase et Roger Ferriter.
1969 Fonde avec le dessinateur suisse Etienne Delessert les «Good Books, Inc.», pour la publication de livres et d'essais publicitaires.
1970 Une agence typographique est créée avec Aaron Burns. Agence à Londres avec Douglas Maxwell.
1971 Agence à Paris avec Robert Delpire.

Professeur à la «Cornell School of Architecture» et conseiller de la «Cooper Union» et du «Hampshire College».
Nombreuses distinctions dans le domaine de la typographie, du graphisme et de la télévision, décernées par le «Type Directors Club», «Art Directors Club» et l'industrie, dont le «Award for Professional Achievement» de la «Sudler & Hennessey, Inc.» et la «Augustus St. Gaudens Medal»; quatre médailles d'or, un «Clio» et le titre de «Art Director of the Year».
Travaux exposés aux Etats-Unis ainsi qu'en Angleterre, France et Allemagne.

1918 Born in New York City.
1939 Graduated from The Cooper Union School of Art and Architecture.
1945 Creative director and vice-president, Sudler & Hennessey, and director of their design organization, Sudler Hennessey & Lubalin.
1964 President of Herb Lubalin, Inc., a design firm.
1968 With Ernie Smith, Tom Carnase, and Roger Ferriter, established Lubalin, Smith, Carnase, Inc.
1969 With the Swiss illustrator Etienne Delessert, established a book production and publishing venture, Good Books, Inc.
1970 With Aaron Burns, established a typographics agency, Lubalin, Burns & Co., Inc. With Douglas Maxwell, established a London studio, Lubalin Maxwell.
1971 With Robert Delpire, established a Paris studio, Lubalin Delpire.

Has taught graphics at Cornell University School of Architecture; serves on the advisory boards of The Cooper Union and Hampshire College.
Member of AIGA, Alliance Graphique Internationale, Nordiska Tecknare (the association of Scandinavian commercial artists), Safft (the Swedish association of graphic designers), Type Directors Club, and the Typographic Center for the Graphic Arts. Has served on panels of AIGA, the IAA World Congress, New York Art Directors Club, and Type Directors Club.
His work has been exhibited in New York and in various European countries. He was named art director of the year in 1962 and received the Clio for the best television commercial in 1963.

1918 In New York geboren.
1939 Besteht Abschlußprüfung der «Cooper Union School of Arts and Architecture».
1945 Ernennung zum Vizepräsidenten der «Sudler & Hennessey, Inc.» sowie zum Creative Director und Direktor der graphischen Abteilung der «SH & L».
1964 Präsident der «Herb Lubalin, Inc.».
1968 Gründet mit Ernie Smith, Tom Carnase und Roger Perriter, die «Lubalin, Smith, Carnase, Inc.».
1969 Gründet mit dem schweizer Illustrator Etienne Delessert die «Good Books, Inc.», die publizistische Versuche und Bücher veröffentlicht.
1970 Agentur für Typographie mit Aaron Burns. Agentur in London mit Douglas Maxwell.
1971 Agentur in Paris mit Robert Delpire.

Professor an der «Cornell School of Architecture» und Berater der «Cooper Union School of Art and Architecture» und des «Hampshire College».
Mitglied amerikanischer und internationaler Gesellschaften für graphische Kunst und Typographie. Gründungsmitglied einer neuen internationalen Organisation, der «International Academy of Communication Arts & Science».
Zahlreiche Auszeichnungen für hervorragende Typographie, Graphik und Fernsehwerbung, die ihm vom «Type Directors Club» und von der Industrie verliehen wurden, darunter der «Award for Professional Achievement» der Sudler & Hennessey, Inc. und die «Augustus St. Gaudens Medal»; insgesamt vier Goldmedaillen, ein «Clio» sowie der Titel «Art Director of the Year». Ausstellungen seiner Arbeiten in den U.S.A., in England, Frankreich und Deutschland.

Herb Lubalin

Herb Lubalin

spa
offe
ingo
For a
write

SH&L Expanded-redesign of
a familiar face. A more flex-
ible version of S&H, long
a favorite of people who
work with fine design.
You can specify SH&L for
a wide range of uses from small
large corporate image projects. We
impact), Oblique (new ways of view-
Casual (no straining for mere effect).
l Herb Lubalin at PLaza 1-1250, or
30 E. 59th Street, New York 20, N.Y.

1

NY, NY

2

M&THER CHILD

3

44

4

fact

5

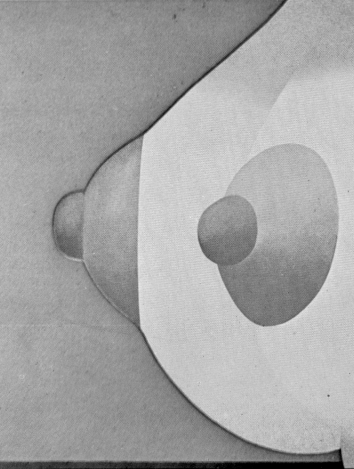

AVANT GARDE

3

Revaluation of the Dollar: 19 Artists Design a New One-Dollar Bill

AVANT GARDE

8

chemical engineering

9

The Saturday Evening Post

10

Hampshire College

11

"Brain Damage"
SORCERY AS AN ART

Ira Cohen and Bill Devore are alchemists of the unconscious, their philosopher's stone a simple 35mm still camera. With a mad genius for costumes and staging, and a technical virtuosity verging on the occult, they created the nightmare suite called "Brain Damage," which follows on the next eight pages. To all appearances, these veteran avant-gardists have incidentally given birth to a brand new art form — located somewhere between photography and painting, cinema and theater. The term "slide production" describes it, without, however, hinting at its poetic extravagance and poisonous beauty. Cohen, a sometime resident of Morocco and expert on exotic drugs, cites the influence of Chinese movies and Marvel comic books; plus the inspiration of underground filmmaker Jack ("Flaming Creatures") Smith. The beguiling monsters of "Brain Damage" are characters in a surrealist epic whose content is what you see in it. They have names such as Dr. Mook, Leon Neon, and The Mojoan Traveler. Like Rorschach tests, they defy you to make out what they mean and what they are up to. But the monsters in "Brain Damage" should not seem so strange. After all, you have met them before — in your wildest dreams!

fact:

JANUARY-FEBRUARY 1964 • VOLUME ONE, ISSUE ONE • $1.25

Bertrand Russell considers *Time* magazine to be "scurrilous and utterly shameless in its willingness to distort." **Ralph Ingersoll:** "In ethics, integrity, and responsibility, *Time* is a monumental failure." **Irwin Shaw:** *Time* is "nastier than any other magazine of the day." **Sloan Wilson:** "Any enemy of *Time* is a friend of mine." **Igor Stravinsky:** "Every music column I have read in *Time* has been distorted and inaccurate." **Tallulah Bankhead:** "Dirt is too clean a word for *Time*." **Mary McCarthy:** "*Time*'s falsifications are numerous." **Dwight Macdonald:** "The degree of credence one gives to *Time* is inverse to one's degree of knowledge of the situation being reported on." **David Merrick:** "There is not a single word of truth in *Time*." **P.G. Wodehouse:** "*Time* is about the most inaccurate magazine in existence." **Rockwell Kent:** *Time* "is inclined to value smartness above truth." **Eugene Burdick:** *Time* employs "dishonest tactics." **Conrad Aiken:** "*Time* slants its news." **Howard Fast:** *Time* provides "distortions and inaccuracies by the bushel." **James Gould Cozzens:** "My knowledge of inaccuracies in *Time* is first-hand." **Walter Winchell:** "*Time*'s inaccuracies are a staple of my column." **John Osborne:** "*Time* is a vicious, dehumanizing institution." **Eric Bentley:** "More pervasive than *Time*'s outright errors is its misuse of truth." **Vincent Price:** "Fortunately, most people read *Time* for laughs and not for facts." **H. Allen Smith:** "*Time*'s inaccuracies are as numerous as the sands of the Sahara." **Taylor Caldwell:** "I could write a whole book about *Time* inaccuracies." **Sen. John McClellan:** "*Time* is prejudiced and unfair."

14

fact:

VOLUME TWO, ISSUE ONE • $1.25

" **The Star Spangled Banner is just so much trash. –Joan Baez** **"** Westbrook Pegler: "I think The Star-Spangled Banner is just terrible." Louis Untermeyer: "The poets and composers of America could come up with something much better." Richard Rodgers: "It's impossible to sing." Marya Mannes: "Any musician will tell you it's a lousy piece of music." Meredith Willson: "It violates every single principle of song writing." Elmer Bernstein: "In today's world, we could do without warlike anthems like The Star-Spangled Banner." Godfrey Cambridge: "It has no meaning for the black man." LeRoi Jones: "It's pompous, hypocritical, vapid, and sterile." Fannie Hurst: "The Star-Spangled Banner, long may it not wave!"

15

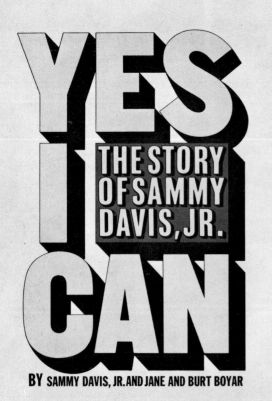

16

17

ALL ANIMALS ARE EQUAL, BUT SOME ANIMALS ARE MORE EQUAL THAN OTHERS.

GEORGE ORWELL
(1903-1950)

A Great Year...
69
Any Way You Look At It

Yes, '69 promises to be a great year (any way you look at it) and one of the things we're looking forward to is a new page every month from the magnificent calendar that appears on the next 12 pages. It is the creation of two brilliant young New York photographers named Steve Horn and Norm Griner, The Horn/Griner Calendar (sometimes referred to as "The Horny Griner Calendar") has by now become something of an institution in the field of commercial art. For six years Messrs. Horn and Griner have been creating their calendars, basing them upon historical events (and non-events), and distributing them free to some 2,000 privileged characters in art studios, ad agencies, museums, etc., across the land. Despite all sorts of juicy offers, Messrs. Horn and Griner have steadfastly refused to permit distribution of their calendars to the general public, preferring that the calendars remain a special treat for persons within the art world. On the theory that readers of Avant-Garde are really as much a part of that world as anyone, however, Messrs. Horn and Griner have kindly consented to the appearance of their latest calendar upon our pages. For which the editors of Avant-Garde would like to publicly express their gratitude (and yours, too, we hope).

La Belle Otero, the famous courtesan of the nineteenth century, was barred from the casino at Monte Carlo for three days when, after losing over a million francs in a mere 12 hours and the croupier having refused her credit on her gold purse, she romped up on the roulette table, ripped off her dress and demanded of him, "What's this worth, cochon?"

'69 JANUARY '69

S	M	T	W	T	F	S
			1	2	3	4
5	6	7	8	9	10	11
12	13	14	15	16	17	18
19	20	21	22	23	24	25
26	27	28	29	30	31	

19

(subjects) — was pejoratively to offend and tease audience susceptibilities.

The four-letter words, the lightness regarding bodily functions, the nudity, the acceptance of adolescent drug-taking, the anti-Establishment attitudes, the mockery of patriotism — these are not the honest ingredients of a Broadway hit.

Yet curiously enough — at least looking back with the benefit of hindsight — the success of Hair was inevitable, and the actual production of Hair a very valuable battle that Broadway had to win.

The battle itself is simple enough. The reason has been artistically the most successful that the Broadway theater has enjoyed in many imports, such as Rosencrantz and Guildenstern Are Dead, the Egg, The Prime of Miss Jean Brodie, even the short-lived Soldiers, have joined such homegrown plays as The Price, Plaza Suite and Scuffold. But note the phrase, "artistically the most successful," for it is sticking in the craw of every producer and every investor along the great white and dirty way, for economically, the times have been hard.

The reason for the gap between artistic, biographic and economic achievement

having slept. (There is network chum, Mimie Pierce and Hamlet later, Left, Jennifer Darling Darcelle, in foreground Couple, Go. "knocked" up by some rowdy, armed freak... amps a long to do ballroom.

31

20

54

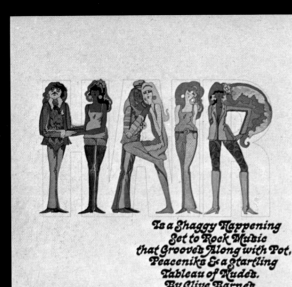

HAIR

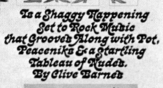

Is a Shaggy Happening Set to Rock Music that Grooved Along with Pot, Peaceniks & a Startling Tableau of Nudes. By Clive Barnes

PHOTOGRAPHS BY PETE TURNER

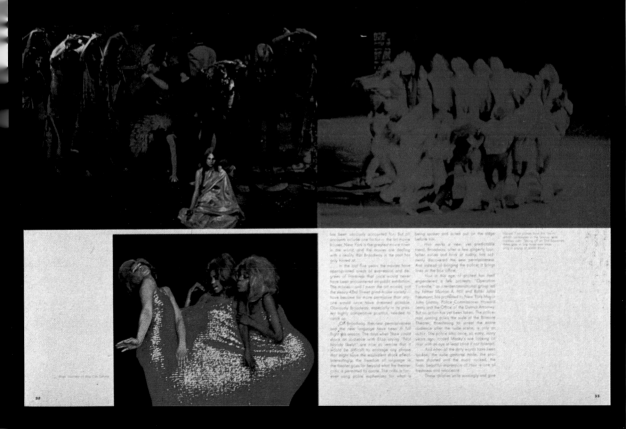

MAURICE CHEVALIER **Old Age Isn't So Bad When You Consider the Alternat_ve**

23

IT'S HARD TO BE HIP OVER THIRTY AND OTHER TRAGEDIES OF MARRIED LIFE

JUDITH VIORST

24

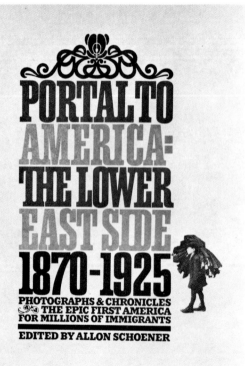

PORTAL TO AMERICA: THE LOWER EAST SIDE 1870-1925
PHOTOGRAPHS & CHRONICLES
THE EPIC FIRST AMERICA
FOR MILLIONS OF IMMIGRANTS
EDITED BY ALLON SCHOENER

25

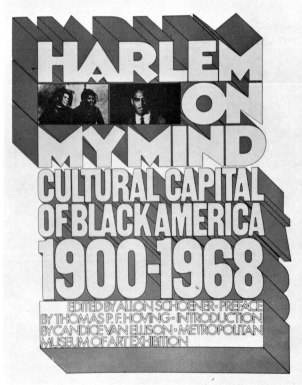

HARLEM ON MY MIND CULTURAL CAPITAL OF BLACK AMERICA 1900-1968
EDITED BY ALLON SCHOENER · PREFACE
BY THOMAS P. F. HOVING · INTRODUCTION
BY CANDICE VAN ELLISON · METROPOLITAN
MUSEUM OF ART EXHIBITION

26

MARRIAGE

27

C.O.D.

NCB
National City Bank
Check&
Charge

28

29

30

31

2

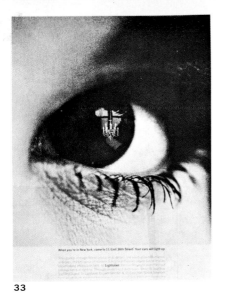

When you're in New York, come to 11 East 36th Street. Your eyes will light up

33

Some of our best friends are bigots.

Ebony.
The magazine that
gets to the heart
of the Negro market.

34

Design by Lubalin.
Photo Engraving by Pioneer-Moss.
Body by Fischer.

35

When was the last time you saw a cotton-pickin' Negro?

Ebony.
The magazine that
gets to the heart
of the Negro market.

36

"She was one of the most unappreciated people in the world."
Joshua Logan, director

39

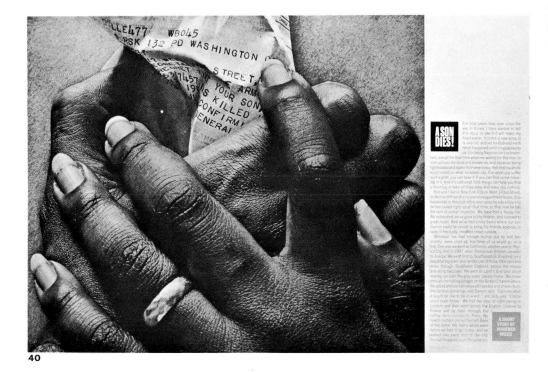

40

A Big Fish Story

This isn't a fable about a chicken. It's a true story about a fish. Its name is Breast-O'-Chicken tuna..

It all started last spring when sales of Breast-O'-Chicken (and other canned tunas) slumped badly. To turn the tide, the Westgate-California Corporation bought one 10-minute segment a week in "Arthur Godfrey Time." Just one a week... and it was the only national advertising for this product in 1963.

Arthur Godfrey started talking about Breast-O'-Chicken tuna on May 28th. Here's what happened—in the words of Milton F. Fillius, Jr., Executive Vice-President: "I am pleased to report that business is looking very good indeed...August and September showed an 80 to 100% improvement in share of market over the same period in 1962. We have concluded (and reports from the field bear it out) that your efforts on our behalf are responsible for a very substantial amount of our improvement."

And that's not the end of the story. Breast-O'-Chicken tuna and Godfrey will be together all of next year.

If you have a good product that's getting lost in a sea of good products, speak to Arthur Godfrey. Whatever you sell, you'll probably have a Big Fish Story to tell—one that really happened.

THE CBS RADIO NETWORK

41

oh!
li-lian oh, representative!
1034 lexington avenue, new york 10021.
murray hill 6-0431

ah!
anthony hyde, jr., photography!
1034 lexington avenue, new york 10021.
murray hill 6-0431

anthony hyde, jr., photography!
1034 lexington avenue, new york 10021.
murray hill 6-0431

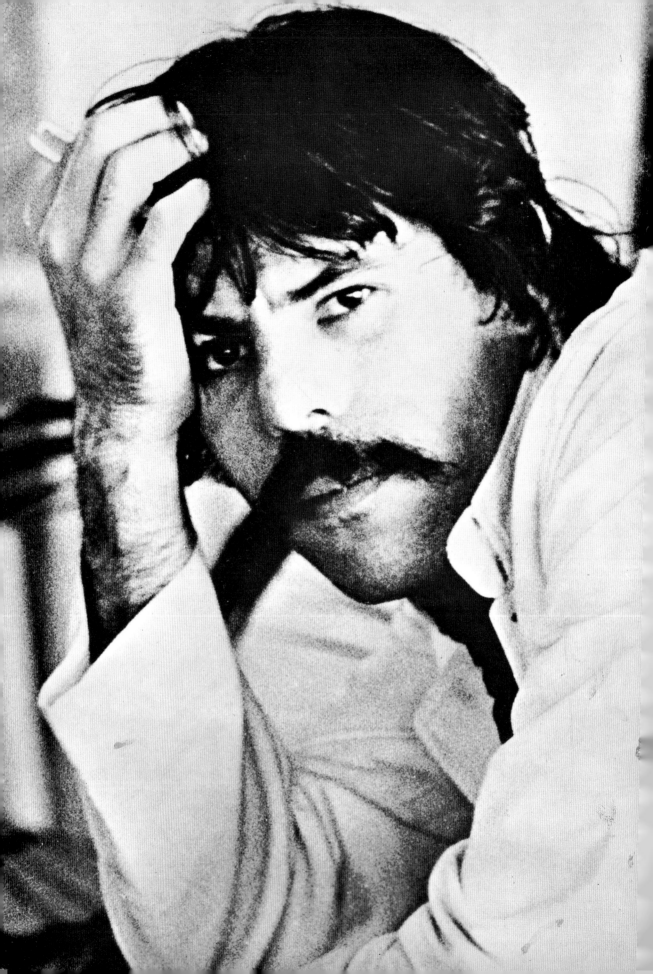

peter max

Peter Max

L'explosion de la Seconde Guerre mondiale, telle est la première rencontre de Peter Max avec la vie. Cette explosion le transporte de Berlin jusqu'à la Chine magique. Son enfance à Chang-Hai, où il vit paisiblement avec sa famille pendant douze ans, est imprégnée par les sons et les visions d'une des cultures les plus anciennes. Au contact d'un monastère bouddhiste proche de a demeure, il s'éveille au monde artistique et spirituel de l'Orient: le son des cloches appelant les religieux à la prière, les incantations, le spectacle fascinant des moines s'initiant à l'art délicat de la peinture, se fixent à jamais dans son jeune esprit.

La famille séjourne ensuite quelque temps au Tibet, voyage autour du monde et en 1949 s'installe en Israël. A Haïfa, Peter Max étudie l'art et l'astronomie. «Je voulais devenir astronome; les galaxies, le cosmos, les années-lumière, cette immensité abstraite du temps et de l'espace me fascinaient». Cette fascination se reflète aujourd'hui dans son œuvre.

En 1953, la famille se déplace à nouveau, passe à Paris et à Rome,

Life met Peter Max in Berlin shortly before World War II exploded—an explosion that carried him to the magical land of China. He spent his childhood in Shanghai, where he lived peacefully with his family for twelve years, immersed in the sights and sounds of one of the most advanced cultures in the world. Living next door to a Buddhist monastery awakened him to the artistic and intellectual world of the East. The sound of bells calling the faithful to prayer, the incantations, the fascinating sight of monks learning the delicate art of the artist's brush were all marked indelibly on his young mind.

In 1949, after a three-month trip around the world, the family settled for a time on Mount Carmel in the port city of Haifa, where Peter studied art with an Austrian professor. At the age of 13, he enrolled in the local university to study astronomy. "I wanted to be an astronomer. The galaxies, the cosmos, the light years—all these abstract distances and time spans fascinated me." This fascination with astronomy is reflected in his art today.

Für Peter Max bedeutet der Ausbruch des Zweiten Weltkrieges die erste Konfrontation mit dem Leben. Die Ereignisse verschlagen ihn von Berlin ins magische China. In Schanghai, wo seine Familie 12 Jahre lang lebt, verbringt er eine von den Tönen und Bildern fernöstlicher Kultur geprägte Kindheit. Der Kontakt mit den Mönchen eines benachbarten buddhistischen Klosters erweckt in ihm die künstlerische und geistige Welt des Ostens. Der Klang der Glocken, der die Gläubigen zum Gebet ruft, die Beschwörungen, das faszinierende Ritual der Mönche, die in die feine Kunst des Pinsels eingeweiht werden — dies alles prägt sich ihm für immer ein.

Nach einem längeren Aufenthalt in Tibet und einer Weltreise wird die Familie im Jahre 1949 in Israel ansässig. In Haifa studiert Peter Kunst und Astronomie. «Ich wollte Astronom werden. Die Galaxien, der Kosmos, die Lichtjahre, diese abstrakte Unermeßlichkeit von Zeit und Raum faszinierten mich.» Diese Faszination spiegelt sich noch heute in seinem Werk.

1953 verlegt die Familie ihren

Peter Max

part finalement pour New York, où Peter Max s'imagine «qu'il vivra au sommet de l'Empire State Building et ira peut-être travailler à l'observatoire du mont Palomar». Ses études secondaires terminées, il fréquente pendant cinq ans plusieurs écoles d'art réputées de New York, la «Art Students League», le «Pratt Graphics Center», et la «School of Visual Arts». Il y acquiert une solide culture artistique. A cette époque, sa femme Liz met au monde deux enfants qui reçoivent les noms célestes de Adam Cosmo et Libra Astral. En 1962, le «Daly-Max Design Studio» est créé. L'original de son portrait de Toulouse-Lautrec pour la biographie de H. Perruchot — qui devint plus tard son premier poster — date de cette période.

Alors que sa carrière publicitaire est à son apogée, Peter Max éprouve le besoin impérieux de s'engager plus profondément dans la recherche de son moi artistique. Il sent «qu'une formidable force créatrice est sur le point de s'exprimer». Il abandonne son studio devenu célèbre et s'installe dans sa résidence actuelle à Riverside Drive, New York City. Pendant deux ans d'isolement dans un monde d'explosions graphiques et de visions cosmiques, 4500 dessins et une nouvelle philosophie esthétique voient le jour.

L'un des buts de Peter Max — transformer le monde entier en galerie de peinture — se réalise partiellement le 30 mars 1969. Ce jour-là, considéré comme une étape décisive, 66 000 bus reproduisent dans 140 villes sa nouvelle conception artistique, qu'il définit comme un «art cosmique en mouvement» (Cosmic Art in Transit). «Le seul message que je voudrais transmettre, c'est ma propre vision des symboles de paix, amour, joie et évolution. J'aimerais apporter la couleur aux grandes villes où les gens sont forcés de vivre dans le chrome, le ciment et le plastique. L'art «en mouvement» doit exciter

After brief stays in Rome and Paris in 1953, the family moved to New York, where Peter hoped he would live on top of the Empire State Building and eventually go to work at the Mount Palomar Observatory in California. After graduating from high school he spent the next five years studying art at the Art Students League, the Pratt Graphics Center, and the School of Visual Arts. During that period Peter Max and his wife Liz became the parents of two children who were given the space-age names of Adam Cosmo and Libra Astral. In 1962, the Daly-Max Design Studio burst upon the advertising world. During the two-year period of its existence, Max made the original design for the book cover of Henri Perruchot's biography of Toulouse-Lautrec, which he later reworked for his first poster. During that period, as well, he won 68 awards for excellence in typography, illustration, and design.

At the peak of his advertising career Max felt a great need for deeper investigation of his artistic self. "I felt a tremendous reservoir of creativity was on the verge of being tapped." He closed his successful studio and moved into his present home on Riverside Drive in New York. During two years of isolation in a world of graphic explosions and cosmic visions, 4500 designs and a new philosophy of aesthetics were born. In 1966, while in Paris working on a movie, Peter Max met the great master of yoga Swami Satchidananda. The experience was an enlightening one and eventually resulted in the formation of the Integral Yoga Institute in New York.

One of Max's aims—to transform the entire world into a picture gallery—was partly realized on 30 March 1969. On that date, which he considers a milestone in his career, 66 000 buses in more than a hundred cities carried re-

Wohnsitz zunächst nach Paris, dann nach Rom und übersiedelt schließlich nach New York, wo Peter glaubt, er werde «im obersten Stockwerk des Empire State Building wohnen und vielleicht im Mount-Palomar-Observatorium arbeiten». Nach bestandenem Abschlußexamen der High School besucht er 5 Jahre lang renommierte New Yorker Kunstschulen, so die «Art Students League», das «Pratt Graphics Center» und die «School of Visual Arts». Er erfährt dort eine ebenso vielseitige wie gründliche künstlerische Ausbildung. Zu dieser Zeit schenkt ihm seine Frau Liz zwei Kinder, die die Himmels-Namen Adam Cosmo und Libra Astral erhalten. Im Jahre 1962 wird das «Daly-Max Design Studio» gegründet. Aus dieser Zeit stammt der Entwurf für den Buchumschlag der Toulouse-Lautrec-Biographie von H. Perruchot. Den Entwurf verwendete er später für sein erstes Poster.

Auf dem Höhepunkt seines Erfolges als Werbegraphiker empfindet Peter Max das unabweisliche Bedürfnis, die Suche nach dem eigenen künstlerischen Ich zu intensivieren. Er spürt, daß eine «gewaltige, schöpferische Kraft auf dem Wege ist, sich zu entfalten». Er schließt sein Studio und richtet sich in seiner heutigen Wohnung am Riverside Drive in Manhattan ein. Zwei Jahre der Abgeschiedenheit in einer Welt graphischer Eruptionen und kosmischer Visionen lassen 4500 Zeichnungen und eine neue ästhetische Philosophie entstehen.

Die ganze Welt in eine Bildergalerie zu verwandeln, gehört zu Peter Max' erklärten Zielen. Ein entscheidender Schritt auf dem Weg zur Verwirklichung dieses Ziels wird am 30. März 1969 zurückgelegt: An diesem Tag — dem, wie er meint, wichtigsten Datum seines künstlerischen Werdegangs — werden Reproduktionen seines neuartigen Schaffens, das er als «bewegte kosmische

Peter Max

le nerf optique: les bus ne sont pas seuls à se déplacer, l'œil du spectateur se meut avec eux. Façon nouvelle d'apprécier l'art, un art qui touche les gens où qu'ils soient. Il n'est plus nécessaire d'aller dans une galerie et de contempler tranquillement une peinture statique». L'art est partout et toute surface vierge est une œuvre d'art en puissance.

L'art cosmique, semblable à l'Art Nouveau et à l'art oriental, s'inspire de la nature et de sa structure. Les motifs floraux symétriques, fréquents dans les peintures de Max, en sont un exemple. L'aspect organique de la nature est une source d'inspiration infinie pour lui: «J'essaie de transposer mes idées en formes et en couleurs qui s'harmonisent avec la nature. C'est dans la nature que l'on trouve les plus belles choses: la fleur, le corps et le visage humains, les écailles du poisson, les galaxies; tous sont ordonnés selon une géométrie vivante, l'évolution, qui est l'unique loi à laquelle la nature se soumet».

Cette loi de l'évolution, Peter Max l'applique aux couleurs du spectre solaire. Pour le fond de ses dessins, il mélange graduellement les couleurs qui se transforment ainsi en d'autres couleurs. Cet effet visuel,

productions of his new art form known as "cosmic art in transit". "The only message I want to convey is my own personal vision of the symbols of peace, love, joy, and evolution. I would like to bring color into the big cities, where people are forced to live among chromium, cement, and plastics. Art 'in transit' is intended to stimulate the optic nerve. It is not only the buses that move; the eye of the onlooker moves with them. This is a new way of appreciating art, an art that reaches people wherever they are. It is no longer necessary to go to a gallery and look at a static painting in peace." Art is everywhere, and every virgin surface is a potential work of art.

Cosmic art, like Art Nouveau and oriental art, takes its inspiration from nature and its structures. Symmetrical floral designs, which are frequent in Max's paintings, are an example of this. The organic aspect of nature is a source of infinite inspiration for him. "I try to transpose my ideas into forms and colors that harmonize with nature. It is in nature that the most beautiful things are to be found—flowers, the human body and face, the scales of a fish, the galaxies; all these things are arranged in accordance with a living geometry, evolution, which is the sole law to which nature is submitted." Peter Max applies this law of evolution to the colors of the solar spectrum. For the backgrounds of his designs, he gradually merges colors and thus transforms them into other colors. He believes that the visual effect thus produced has a calming effect on the nervous system.

Religion, mythology, and oriental symbolism are frequently found in Max's designs. His poster "Coach with the Six Insides" represents a Tibetan demon in the form of a Buddhist mandala. "The oriental peoples have their own symbols—demons, flowers. the symmetry of

Kunst» (cosmic art in transit) bezeichnet, in insgesamt 66 000 in 140 Städten verkehrenden Bussen gezeigt. «Die einzige Botschaft, welche ich übermitteln möchte, ist meine Vision der Symbole für Frieden, Liebe, Freude und Weiterentwicklung. Ich möchte Farbe in die großen Städte bringen, wo die Menschen gezwungen sind, zwischen Chrom, Zement und Kunststoff zu leben. Die *bewegte* Kunst soll den optischen Nerv erregen. Nicht der Bus allein bewegt sich, das Auge des Betrachters bewegt sich mit ihm. Es geht um eine neue Art, Kunst zu genießen, eine Kunst, welche die Leute unmittelbar anrührt, wo immer sie sich befinden. Es ist nicht mehr nötig, in eine Galerie zu gehen und in Ruhe ein statisches Gemälde zu betrachten. Die Kunst ist überall, und jede unberührte Fläche ist ein potentielles Kunstwerk.»

Die kosmische Kunst wird, ähnlich dem Jugendstil und der östlichen Kunst, von der Natur und ihren Strukturen inspiriert. Die symmetrischen Blütenmotive, welche auf den Blättern von Peter Max so häufig wiederkehren, sind ein Beispiel dafür. Der organische Aspekt der Natur ist für ihn Quelle unbegrenzter Inspiration. «Ich versuche, meine Ideen in Formen und Farben umzuwandeln, welche mit der Natur harmonisieren. Die schönsten Dinge sind in der Natur zu finden: die Blumen, der Leib und das Antlitz des Menschen, die Schuppen des Fisches, die Galaxien. Sie alle sind nach einer lebendigen Geometrie geformt, der Geometrie der Evolution, die das einzige Gesetz ist, dem die Natur gehorcht.» Dieses Gesetz der Evolution wendet Peter Max auf die Farben des Sonnenspektrums an. Dem visuellen Effekt seiner farbig abgestuften Bildgründe schreibt er eine beruhigende Wirkung auf das Nervensystem des Betrachters zu.

Die Religion, die Mythologie und der Symbolismus des Fernen Ostens sind in seinen Zeichnungen

Peter Max

pense-t-il, a un effet calmant sur le système nerveux.

La religion, la mythologie et le symbolisme orientaux sont souvent présents dans les dessins de Max. Son poster «Coach With the Six Insides» représente le démon tibétain Diety sous forme de mandala bouddhiste. «Les peuples orientaux ont leurs symboles: le démon, la fleur, la symétrie de leurs dessins. Ceux de la nouvelle culture américaine des années 60 sont des mots comme «Amour» et «Paix». Celui des années 70 sera «Cosmologie». La pensée orientale se développe sans cesse depuis 4000 ans. Aujourd'hui seulement il y a échange entre l'Est et l'Ouest; nous faisons profiter l'Est de nos progrès technologiques et nous recevons, en retour, sa pensée mystique. Il appartient aux artistes, aux écrivains et aux musiciens du monde entier d'ensemencer cette spiritualité en chaque être humain moderne. C'est seulement de cette manière que nous pourrons évoluer et que notre époque pourra atteindre glorieusement l'âge d'or».

their designs. Those of the new American culture of the sixties are words like 'love' and 'peace'. That of the seventies will be 'cosmology'. Oriental thought has been developing without pause for 4000 years. But today, for the first time, there is an interchange between East and West. We are allowing the East to profit from our technological progress and we receive, in return, its mystical thought. It is the task of artists, writers, and musicians all over the world to implant this mentality in every modern human being. Only in this way shall we be capable of evolving, and only thus shall we be able to make this a glorious golden age.''

gegenwärtig. Sein Poster «Coach with the Six Insides» stellt einen tibetanischen Dämon in Form einer buddhistischen Mandala dar. «Die fernöstlichen Völker haben ihre eigenen Symbole: Dämonen, Blumen, die Symmetrie ihrer Formen. Die Symbole der neuen amerikanischen Kultur der sechziger Jahre sind Wörter wie *Liebe* und *Frieden*. Das Symbol der siebziger Jahre wird *Kosmologie* sein. Fernöstliches Denken ist das Ergebnis einer 4000jährigen ununterbrochenen Entwicklung. Erst heute ist es zum Austausch zwischen Ost und West gekommen. Wir lassen den Osten an unserem technologischen Fortschritt teilhaben und empfangen dafür sein mystisches Gedankengut. Aufgabe der Künstler, der Schriftsteller und der Musiker der ganzen Welt ist es, diesen Geist in jedem modernen Menschen wachzurufen. Nur auf diese Weise werden wir uns fortschreitend weiterentwickeln und hoffen können, in unserer Epoche das *Goldene Zeitalter* heraufkommen zu sehen».

Peter Max

1937	Né à Berlin.		*1937*	*Born in Berlin.*		1937	In Berlin geboren.
1939	Sa famille s'établit à Chang-Hai.		*1939*	*Family settled in Shanghai.*		1939	Übersiedlung seiner Familie nach Schanghai.
1949	Voyage autour du monde avec ses parents.		*1949*	*Traveled around the world with his parents.*		1949	Weltreise mit seinen Eltern.
1950	Etudie l'astronomie et l'art à Haïfa.		*1950*	*Studied art and astronomy in Haifa.*		1950	Studium der Astronomie und der Kunst in Haifa.
1953	Part pour New York, où il étudie à l'«Art Students League», au «Pratt Graphics Center» et à la «School of Visual Arts».		*1953*	*Came to New York, where he studied at the Art Students League, the Pratt Graphics Center, and the School of Visual Arts.*		1953	Übersiedlung nach New York. Studium an der «Art Students League», am «Pratt Graphics Center» und an der «School of Visual Arts».
1962	Crée le «Daly-Max Design Studio» avec son ami Daly.		*1962*	*Set up the Daly-Max Design Studio with his friend Daly.*		1962	Gründung des «Daly-Max Design Studio» mit seinem Freund Daly.
1964	S'établit comme créateur indépendant à Riverside Drive, New York.		*1964*	*Set up as an independent creative artist on Riverside Drive in New York.*		1964	Etabliert sich als freier Gestalter am Riverside Drive in Manhattan.
1966	Rencontre à Paris le Swami Satchidananda, illustre maître de yoga.		*1966*	*While in Paris, met Swami Satchidananda, the master of yoga.*		1966	Begegnet Swami Satchidananda, dem berühmten Yoga-Meister, in Paris.
1970	Président de la société Peter Max.		*1970*	*Became president of Peter Max Company.*		1970	Präsident der Firma Peter Max. Arbeitet als «Graphic Designer».

Nombreuses distinctions dans le domaine de la typographie, de l'art graphique et du «Design».

Has received many distinctions in the fields of typography, graphic art, and design.

Zahlreiche Auszeichnungen auf dem Gebiet der Typographie, der graphischen Kunst und des «Design», darunter 68 Preise allein aus den Jahren 1962-1964.

Peter Max

Michael J. Pollard

STAGE 9

peter max

A PLACE TO BE

2

peter max

4

5

peter max

A comedy inspired by James Joyce's "Finnegans Wake"

TRIUMPHANT RETURN FROM WORLD-WIDE SUCCESS! JEAN ERDMAN'S CELEBRATED PRODUCTION

THE COACH WITH THE SIX INSIDES

peter max

ST 74th ST. THEATRE, 334 E. 74th St. (Bet. 1st & 2nd Aves.), N. Y. C. Phone UN 1-2288

7

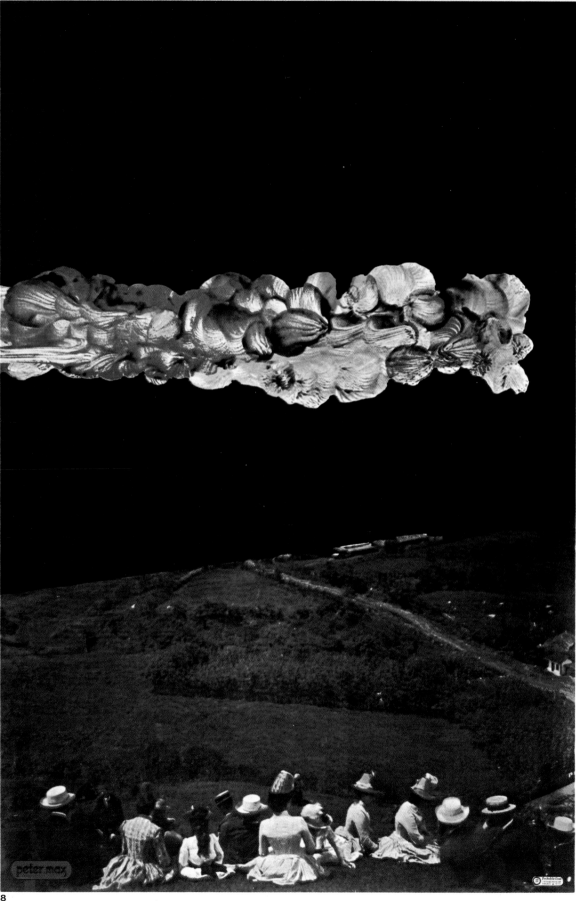

9

"Groovy Noon" Copyright 1968 Peter Max Poster Corporation, New York, N

10

peter max

11

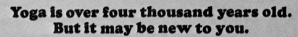

Yoga is over four thousand years old.
But it may be new to you.

Yoga is a scientific system that makes you the master of your senses.
Instead of being a slave to them.

Yoga is not just standing on your head, as many people think,
but learning how to stand on your own two feet.

Yoga is not a religion. Yet it embraces all religions.

Yoga can teach the young the wisdom of age
and teach the old the secret of youth.

Yoga will introduce you to someone you might not know. Your Self.

Swami Satchidananda will introduce you to Yoga.

Swami Satchidananda at the Village Theater. Friday, Sept. 8 at 8 p.m.
A birthday celebration of Sri Swami Sivananda, Himalayas.

12

13

14

15

peter max

peter max

18

21

peter max

23

Henry Wolf

Il y a plus de vingt-deux ans que je suis graphiste à New York. Je déteste les gens qui élaborent des lois générales sur la création, car ils énoncent ordinairement des lieux communs ou se font, d'une manière à peine déguisée, de la publicité. Plutôt que de parler de mon talent ou de celui d'autrui, il me semble plus intéressant de déterminer la nature des obstacles qui empêchent l'immense potentiel de talent recelé dans notre pays d'être exploité et confronté au public.

Rétrospectivement, on ne peut pourtant pas se montrer trop pessimiste: au début de ma carrière, seule une très faible minorité d'agences de publicité et de magazines considérait le talent comme une qualité essentielle pour réussir dans le domaine du graphisme. Les autres le toléraient, ils gardaient un génie en cage et répandaient sa production adaptée à l'usage du grand public. Depuis toujours le génie est en avance sur son temps ou difficilement accessible pour l'homme moyen. Concevoir un produit ou un article de journal pour le grand public, c'est-à-dire

I hate general pronouncements about the state of creativity because they are mostly meaningless axioms or thingly disguised self-promotion. The phenomenon that needs examination is not so much my talent—or anyone else's—but the nature of the obstacle which prevents the enormous reserve of talent that exists here from being released for a confrontation with the public.

The outlook is not altogether pessimistic: When I started working, only a handful of magazines and two or three advertising agencies considered talent in design a real asset. The rest tolerated it. They kept a genius in a cage and watered down his production— "adapted" it for general use. Being a genius has always meant to be ahead of one's time, or not completely in touch and in tune with the "average." That's a big problem when you are in business to sell a product or a magazine article to the great masses who must by definition be more or less "average." The problem still exists and will always exist as long as exceptional vision is used in a

Seit mehr als 22 Jahren bin ich in New York als Graphiker tätig. Ich verabscheue Leute, die allgemeingültige Regeln über das künstlerische Schaffen aufstellen wollen, denn meistens kommen sie dabei über Gemeinplätze nicht hinaus oder machen mehr oder weniger unverhüllt für sich selbst Reklame. Viel interessanter, als über mein Talent oder das anderer zu sprechen, erscheint es mir, die Widerstände zu erörtern, die das in unserem Land brachliegende immense Potential an Talent daran hindern, genutzt und der Öffentlichkeit vorgestellt zu werden.

Im Vergleich zu den Verhältnissen, wie sie zu Beginn meiner Laufbahn herrschten, sollte man die heutige Situation freilich nicht gar zu pessimistisch sehen. Talent wurde damals nur von den wenigsten Werbeagenturen und Zeitschriften als für den Erfolg auf graphischem Gebiet wesentliche Eigenschaft betrachtet. Von anderen wurde es lediglich geduldet. Sie sperrten das Genie in einen — keineswegs immer goldenen — Käfig, «adaptierten» sein Werk für den Bedarf des Publikums und brachten es

Henry Wolf

pour un niveau moyen, pose un problème complexe à l'homme d'affaires. Ce problème a existé et existera aussi longtemps qu'une vision exceptionnelle sera destinée à des gens moyens.

Il y a deux façons d'aborder ce dilemme: on peut soit vulgariser l'idée du créateur de talent — en atténuant l'originalité de son idée, par exemple — soit admettre que la masse n'a pas forcément le goût aussi infantile que le pensaient les grands promoteurs de la publicité il y a dix ans et les éditeurs du temps passé, qui imaginaient l'Amérique au-delà de New York comme un grand terrain de jeu pour adolescents retardés.

Cette révolution du jugement a deux origines. De nombreux «businessmen» ont réalisé des fortunes en donnant au public non pas ce qu'ils pensaient que celui-ci voulait, mais ce qu'ils estimaient qu'il aurait dû avoir. Ils ont fait un bien énorme en rehaussant le niveau du goût moyen, qui n'est plus du tout moyen selon les normes d'antan. Par un juste retour des choses, le public, qui n'a pas été sous-estimé, exige d'avantage. Plus on traite les gens en adultes intelligents, plus ils font preuve de discernement et d'appétits nouveaux. Il en résulte une étrange volte-face. Le monde des affaires n'est plus effrayé par le créateur excentrique, au contraire il le recherche et l'exhibe. L'expert-comptable habitué à faire tampon entre le graphiste ou le directeur artistique et le client est aujourd'hui à la retraite dans son «country club», et le jeune créateur affronte, face à face, le grand industriel. Les vieux clichés, tel le mirage de la souriante et éternellement jeune femme, sont périmés. La publicité traite maintenant de vrais problèmes. La sexualité, inhérente à la vie moderne, n'est plus un tabou, et elle est souvent mise à contribution pour vendre certains produits. Comme l'art cinématographique, la publicité et l'édition sont deve-

mass medium. There are two ways to deal with this discrepancy: The old way was to "popularize" the ideas of the gifted designer, i.e., lower his originality. The new way seems, happily, to assume that the public's taste is not altogether as infantile as assumed by the advertising wizards of ten years ago or the old-time publishers who looked upon the America outside of New York as a large playground of subnormal adolescents.

The revolution is happening from two sides: There are now many gifted entrepreneurs who have made great financial gains from giving the public not what they think it wants but what they think it ought to have. They are doing enormous good in raising the taste level of an "average" that is no longer average by the old standards. The other side is a playback from the public which has not been underestimated and which gratefully screams for more. It is an unvicious circle. The more the masses get treated and talked to as intelligent adults, the more discerning and demanding they become. This has resulted in a strange turnabout: Big business is not afraid of the odd-ball thinker any more. On the contrary, it looks for him and shows him off. The old account man who used to be the go-between to smooth the problems of confrontation between the client and the creative writer or art director has now been all but retired to his country club and young designers are arguing with big industrialists, face-to-face. Advertisements do not use mirages like the smiling, eternally young girl but talk about real problems. Sex is not a delusion but a fact of life, often used for selling products. Like the films, publishing and advertising have become much less unreal, which brings them much closer to the corner of the true artist whose concern has always been self-expression. And self-

unter die Leute. Seit jeher ist das Genie seiner Zeit voraus und für den Durchschnittsbürger schwer verständlich gewesen. Ein Produkt oder einen Zeitungsartikel für die große Öffentlichkeit, d.h. für den «Durchschnittsgeschmack» zu konzipieren, stellt den Geschäftsmann vor ein schwieriges Problem. Dieses Problem hat schon immer bestanden und wird auch weiterhin bestehen, sobald und solange es darum geht, eine außergewöhnliche Vision auf das Niveau des «Durchschnittsgeschmacks» zu projizieren.

Es gibt zwei Möglichkeiten, dieses Dilemma zu lösen: Indem man (und das war die bisher geübte Praxis) die Ideen des talentierten Künstlers gemeinverständlich macht — beispielsweise durch Verminderung ihrer Originalität — oder indem man sich eingesteht, daß die Masse nicht unbedingt jenen infantilen Geschmack haben muß, den ihr die Werbebosse, die vor 10 Jahren regierten, und die Verleger vergangener Zeiten, die meinten, mit Ausnahme von New York sei Amerika ein einziger großer Spielplatz für geistig behinderte Halbwüchsige, zuschrieben. Dieser radikale Wandel in der Beurteilung der Dinge hat zwei Ursachen. Es gibt heute schon eine ganze Reihe von Geschäftsleuten, die ein Vermögen haben, weil sie dem Publikum nicht das gaben, wonach es ihrer Meinung nach verlangte, sondern das, wovon sie annahmen, daß es ihm eigentlich gebühre. Sie haben auf diese Weise viel dazu beigetragen, das Niveau des «Durchschnittsgeschmacks» soweit zu heben, daß er heute keineswegs mehr «durchschnittlich» im Sinne der früheren Normen genannt werden kann. Die natürliche Folge war, daß das in seinem Urteilsvermögen nicht mehr unterschätze Publikum — und dies ist der zweite der für den Wandel ursächlichen Gründe — seinerseits höhere Ansprüche zu stellen begann. Ein ganz und gar nicht

Henry Wolf

nues plus humaines, ce qui les rapproche des aspirations de l'artiste sincère, qui recherche avant tout l'expression personnelle. Cette expression personnelle n'est authentique que si elle rejoint la vérité profonde du dessinateur, sinon elle n'est que falsification.

La falsification ne nourrit plus son homme, elle ne trompe plus personne. C'est le résultat le plus probant, le plus optimiste de cette révolution du jugement.

expression, if it is to be valid, has to be very close to the designer's or writer's sense of truth, otherwise it is a fake or a phony. And the best thing that's happened here is that phoniness no longer gets you anywhere.

teuflischer Circulus vitiosus! Behandelt man die Leute als erwachsene, intelligente Menschen, so erweist sich, daß sie sehr wohl kritisch zu unterscheiden vermögen und nach mehr und Besserem verlangen. Daraus resultiert eine völlige Umkehrung der Situation. Die Geschäftswelt läßt sich von den exzentrischen Künstlern nun nicht mehr abschrecken. Im Gegenteil: Man sucht sie und bringt sie groß heraus.

Der Etatdirektor von ehedem, der es gewohnt war, zwischen dem Graphiker oder dem Art Director einerseits und dem Kunden andererseits als Puffer zu dienen, ist heute noch am ehesten in seinem «Country Club» anzutreffen, während der junge Künstler dem Großindustriellen unmittelbar gegenübertritt. Die alten Klischees, wie das Traumbild der ewig lächelnden, ewig jungen Frau usw., sind verblaßt. Die Werbung greift heute die wirklichen Probleme auf. Die aus dem modernen Leben nicht wegzudenkende Sexualität ist schon lange kein Tabu mehr und wird oft als gestalterisches Mittel gebracht, um für gewisse Produkte zu werben.

Wie die Filmkunst sind heute auch die Werbung und das Verlagswesen menschlicher geworden. Das bringt sie denjenigen Künstlern näher, deren Ziel es vor allem ist, eine eigene Ausdrucksweise zu finden. Diese persönliche Ausdrucksweise ist nur dann authentisch, wenn sie der inneren Wahrheit des Künstlers entspricht. Sonst ist sie nichts als Verfälschung.

Vom Fälschen aber kann heute niemand mehr leben, weil sich die Leute nicht mehr täuschen lassen. Das ist das positivste Ergebnis dieser Entwicklung.

Henry Wolf

1925 Né à Vienne.
1941 S'établit aux Etats-Unis, après avoir étudié à Paris. Effectue deux ans de service militaire dans l'armée américaine.
1944 Travaille dans des agences et pour le «U.S. Department of State».
1952-1958 Nommé directeur artistique du magazine «Esquire», il en recrée toute la conception: format et mise en page.
1958-1961 Nommé directeur artistique du magazine «Haper's Bazaar».
1961-1964 Nommé directeur artistique du magazine «Show», il en revoit toute la conception visuelle.
1964 Nommé directeur artistique de «Jack Tinker & Partners».
1965 Entre au «McCann-Erikson's Center for Advanced Practice».
1966 Nommé «Executive Vice President and Creative Director» de l'agence «Trahey Advertising».
1967 Devient associé de «Trahey Wolf, Inc.».

Membre d'associations américaines et internationales d'art graphique, d'illustrateurs, d'instituts universitaires, il enseigna à la «Cooper Union School» et à la «School of Visual Arts». A plusieurs reprises «Chairman», «Co-Chairman», il est actuellement «Director of the A.I.G.A.» et fut nommé cinq ans consécutifs «Art Director of the Year».
Nombreuses distinctions décernées par les «Art Directors Club», et associations graphiques, dont six médailles.
Ses articles et ses travaux ont paru dans les revues et journaux d'art graphique les plus importants du monde entier.

1925 Born in Vienna.
1941 Came to the United States after having studied in Paris.
1943-46 Military service.
1944 Worked for various advertising agencies and the U.S. Department of State.
1952-58 Art director, "Esquire"; redesigned its format.
1958-61 Art director, "Harper's Bazaar."
1961-64 Art director, "Show"; designed original format.
1964 Art director, Jack Tinker & Partners.
1965 Joined McCann-Erickson's Center for Advanced Practice.
1966 Executive vice-president and creative director, Trahey Advertising.
1967 Partner, Trahey Wolf, Inc.

Taught design at The Cooper Union School of Art and Architecture and the School of Visual Arts, New York.
As a free-lance designer, has been active in publishing and films.
Chairman of 38th Annual Art Directors Who, 1963; guest speaker at the "Eyes West" Symposium of the University of California and at the Visual Communications Conference, New York, 1963; chairman of the Visual Communications Conference, New York, 1968; co-chairman of the International Design Conference, Aspen, 1969 (and remains a director of the conference); president, AIGA; member, Alliance Graphique Internationale; fellow, Royal Society of Arts, London.
Nominated as art director of the year five consecutive times. Received six medals and many awards from the New York Art Directors Club, the AIGA, the Society of Illustrators, and other organizations. Listed in "Who's Who in America" and "Who's Who in Graphic Arts."

1925 In Wien geboren.
1941 Beendigung des Studiums in Paris und Übersiedlung nach den U.S.A. 2 Jahre Militärdienst in der amerikanischen Armee.
1944 Arbeitet in Agenturen und für das amerikanische Außenministerium.
1952-1958 Art Director des «Esquire»-Magazins, Umgestaltung der gesamten Konzeption hinsichtlich Format, Layout, Umbruch.
1958-1961 Art Director der Zeitschrift «Harper's Bazaar».
1961-1964 Art Director des «Show»-Magazins, Neugestaltung der visuellen Konzeption.
1964 Art-Director bei Jack Tinker & Partners.
1965 Eintritt in das «McCann-Erikson's Center for Advanced Practice».
1966 «Executive Vice President and Creative Director» der «Trahey Advertising»-Agentur.
1967 Teilhaber der «Trahey Wolf, Inc.».

Mitglied amerikanischer und internationaler Gesellschaften für graphische Kunst, von Instituten und Universitäten sowie von diversen Illustratoren – Vereinigungen und Verbänden, Lehrer an der «Cooper Union School of Art and Architecture» und an der «School of Visual Arts» in New York. Nach mehrfacher Wiederwahl zum «Chairman» und «Co-Chairman» gegenwärtig «Director of A.I.G.A.». In fünf aufeinanderfolgenden Jahren zum «Art Director of the Year» nominiert.
Zahlreiche Auszeichnungen durch den New Yorker «Art Directors Club» und andere Graphiker-Vereinigungen. Sechs Medaillen.
Seine Artikel und Arbeiten sind in den bedeutendsten internationalen Fachzeitschriften und -blättern erschienen.

Henry Wolf

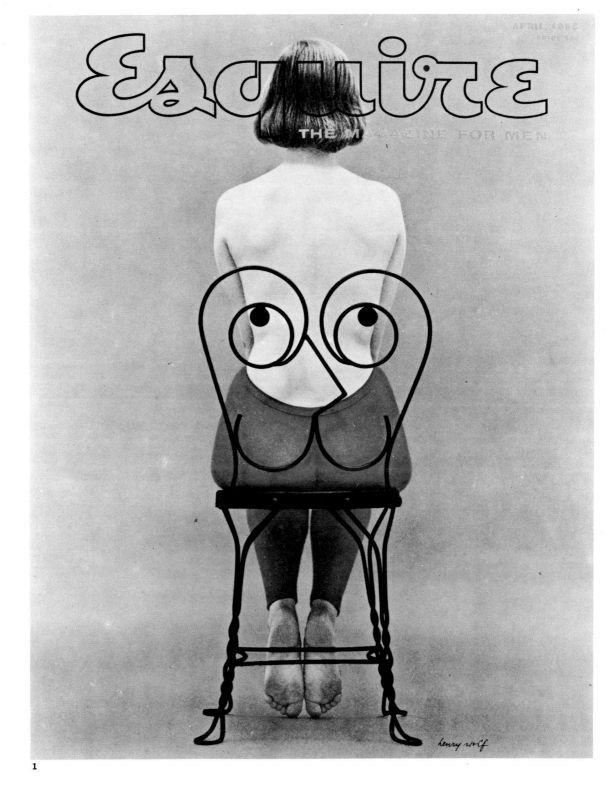

1

2

3

4

6

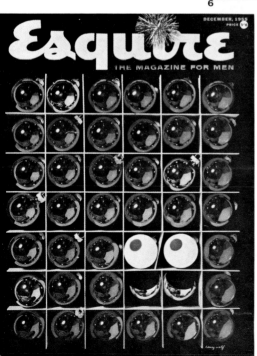

7

8 EQUATORIAL SHADES FROM MANGO TO PAPAYA TO NECTARINE. 2.50 IN A NEW PAGO-PAGO CASE.

Go to the islands.
Buy a mango. Take a bite.
Note the way the fruit
colors your lips.
Natural. Clear. Delicious.
Go buy Elizabeth Arden's
new "Color Clear" lipsticks.
Same thing.

Elizabeth Arden

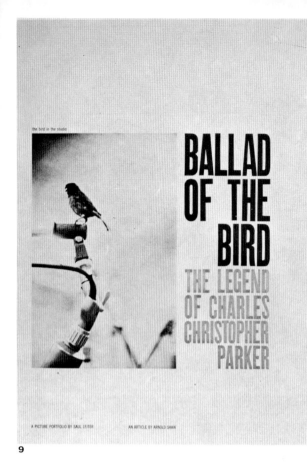

the bird in the studio

BALLAD OF THE BIRD
THE LEGEND OF CHARLES CHRISTOPHER PARKER

A PICTURE PORTFOLIO BY SAUL LEITER   AN ARTICLE BY ARNOLD SHAW

9

the bird's first horn

THE
AUTOMOBILE'S
CLASSIC
DECADES:
A
PORTFOLIO
BY
LESLIE SAALBURG

10

HARPER'S

BAZAAR

THE
WONDERS
OF
WATER

EARLY
MEMOIRS
OF
SIMONE
DE
BEAUVOIR

INSIDER'S
NEW YORK

MAY 1959
60 CENTS

reading,
'riting
and
'rithmetic

Taught to the tune of a teaching machine: a teaching machine that moves the student along as rapidly as he can or as slowly as he needs.

Which is the point behind the whole revolution that's fast changing the face of education in our country.

How else can we provide more and better education for our children, for adults, even for industry, than through automated teaching? And since education costs are soaring right along with a demand for better education, automation seems natural.

But what happens to the teachers? Do they lose their prestige and power? Are they eliminated along with the textbooks?

No. The consensus seems to be that the teacher will be able to teach more effectively and efficiently. They'll actually be more involved with the whole educational output; be able to concentrate more on individual student's problems while others are moving ahead on their own; and, all told, be able to do about twice what they did before.

And the students, what about them? Will they be bored with all these dehumanized gadgets?

No. Again, the consensus seems to indicate that students will be more excited about learning than ever, simply because they will be teaching themselves.

And the textbooks? What happens to them under automated teaching?

Many educators feel that reliance on books will sort of dwindle. Educators point out that the ear and the eye naturally assimilate information much more readily and faster than it's possible to do through the code of written words. (In place of speed-reading, one educator hopes to offer speed listening.)

From simpler devices, we'll make more and more use of computers, which will communicate directly with the student at the same time they make the teacher just that much more efficient.

Today, Ogden participates in education through training the hard core unemployed in Long Island, New York, San Antonio, Oklahoma City, Los Angeles and New Orleans. What we teach are the skills useful in shipbuilding, aircraft construction, hydraulic systems and Ogden's own technology labs. Ogden plans to use its know-how and expertise in research and technology to become more thoroughly involved in our fantastic educational revolution.

A revolution, Ogden believes, that will see happier, better paid teachers, students who become more effective learners, and a really adequate educational system. Not to mention a more responsible, culturally enriched citizenry, that isn't composed of 14 million American adults who now read below the fourth grade level.

Get the picture?

Ogden the anticipator

12

Can an asparagus find happiness with a drill head?

Tune into Ogden and find out. Ogden's happiness quotient with a large food processing company in California and a mining equipment manufacturing company in Utah has been very high and has produced a lovely green child called Money (takes after his mother).

We also have married aircraft parts to hospital supplies, shipbuilding to water filtration, missile testing to lab equipment kits, and offshore drilling rigs to planned industrial sites. So far our matchmaking philosophy has proved to be profitable for all concerned.

In Fortune's last "500 Directory" Ogden had quietly slipped up to 130th place and even though the 1967 figures haven't been tallied yet we know Ogden will be moving up again in the world.

Want to know more about this quiet giant? Write us at 161 East 42d Street, New York, New York 10017.

Ogden Corporation

13

The great Ogden quiz:

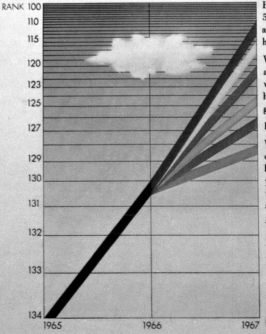

RANK 100 — 134 (rows: 100, 110, 115, 120, 123, 125, 127, 129, 130, 131, 132, 133, 134) across years 1965, 1966, 1967

Before you turn to the Fortune 500 Listing, test your intuition about whether the quiet giant has taken another giant step.

We were 134th two years ago and 130th last year. When this ad went to press the 1967 figures had not been released and your guess may be as good as ours.

But we're optimistic by nature.

Want to know more about this quiet giant? Turn now to the Fortune 500 Listing to check your calculation. Then you migh want to know even more about Ogden. You can if you'll just write us at 161 East 42d Street, New York. New York 10017.

Ogden Corporation

111

OH

BY N. F. SIMPSON

Humphrey: No, Laura, I don't think it's the kind of thing we could expect Graham to show much interest in.

Laura: Oh?

Humphrey: He's very orthodox in many ways. As far as his painting is concerned.

Laura: I need say he doesn't show much preference for orthodox methods in anything else.

Humphrey: All the same, Laura, I think that to fix the brush in a vice and move the canvas about on the end of it would create more problems than it would solve.

Laura: I should have thought it would have been the very thing for Graham.

Humphrey: I'll suggest it to him, of course—but you mustn't be surprised if he turns it down. Don't forget he's got all this line on his mind still about Colonel Padlock's portrait—that must be taking up practically every spare minute of his time.

Laura: What has about Colonel Padlock's portrait? He's finished it. He must have.

Humphrey: He's had a great deal to do, Laura.

Laura: You don't mean to say poor Colonel Padlock is still sitting there? Waiting?

Humphrey: It isn't just a matter of setting an easel up, Laura, and a canvas, and beginning to paint. Just like that.

Laura: I think that's absolutely disgraceful! What for heaven's sake has he been doing?

Humphrey: He hasn't been wasting his time, my dear.

Laura: It must be six weeks since all this started. At least, I can't think what he can have been doing all that time.

Humphrey: So far as I know, Colonel Padlock hasn't complained.

Laura: Why on earth doesn't he get people to help him?

Humphrey: You won't persuade Graham to delegate responsibility, my dear.

Laura: Doing every single thing himself from scratch.

Humphrey: Yes, well, there it is. If he prefers to work that way. . . .

Laura: I'd say nothing if it were simply a matter of constructing his own easels. With homemade glue.

Humphrey: After all.

Laura: Or even weaving his canvases himself. But growing his own hemp, or whatever it is, to do it with! That's carrying it too far!

Humphrey: Yes, well—I'm afraid I side with Graham over this, Laura.

Laura: Felling the timber himself for his brush handles and planing it down till it's small enough.

Humphrey: What other way is there, Laura, if you're determined to keep control over the finished picture? And that's the whole crux of it as far as Graham is concerned. As you know.

Laura: And in the meantime, Colonel Padlock has to sit there.

Humphrey: As far as that goes I should think Colonel Padlock would be the last person to want to see Graham compromise his professional integrity on his account.

Laura: So he just has to sit waiting. While Graham goes all over the world looking for natural pigments and one thing and another.

Humphrey: My dear Laura, what else can he possibly do (Continued on page 229)

For the Carriage Trade—a make-up that expresses an essential feminine paradox in a look both strong and fragile: lips—in a contemporary take-off of the Cupid's bow—are racy red softened with pink (Henry Bendel Bon Bon lipstick, matching nail enamel); eyes—shaded with faint shadow and mascara, in Bluebird; skin—toned with Touch and Glow. All by Revlon. Ring—a sensation composed of one smashing 33-carat canary sapphire, diamond and platinum petals. By Schlumberger at Tiffany

BAZAAR

HARPER'S

THE
BEAUTY
OF
BEING
YOURSELF
IN LOOKS
IN DRESS
IN LIVING

IN THIS ISSUE:
TRUMAN CAPOTE
EDITH SITWELL
ANTHONY WEST

OCTOBER 1959
60 CENTS

7

BAZAAR

HARPER'S

MARCH 1960
60 CENTS

IN
AMERICA:
GREAT
FASHION
IN
MOTION

FOR
BEAUTY:
THREE
FRESH
MAKE-UPS

ON
FOOT:
SHOES
CUT-OUT
FOR
DAY

FROM
PARIS:
THE
NEW
COLLECTIONS

18

BAZAAR

HARPER'S

PRESENTS

AUDREY HEPBURN
MEL FERRER
PARIS PURSUIT

A LOVE FARCE

FEATURING THE PARIS COLLECTIONS

WITH BUSTER KEATON   DIRECTED BY RICHARD AVEDON

PLUS THE AMERICAN FASHION OPENINGS

SEPTEMBER 1959
CENTS

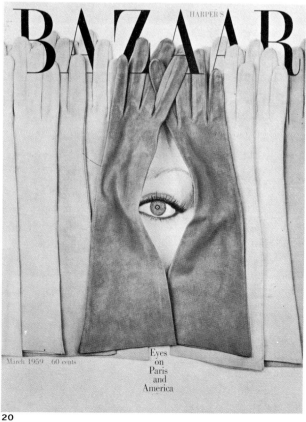

BAZAAR

HARPER'S

March 1959   60 cents

Eyes
on
Paris
and
America

20

JUST HOW FAR CAN A GIRL GO ON A PROMENADE?   WAY OUT.

PROMENADE LTD. IMPORTED KNITWEAR VENICE / IN NEW YORK AT 498 SEVENTH AVENUE

21

The Trigère Cult

2

23

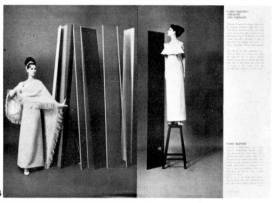

24

25

26

27

SUBLIME
CHILD
BY
GINA
BERRIAULT

oseph Carmody was conspicuousl
and mistress of five years, Alice
their cars in the misty cemetery,
relief, for they had admired him
back to the city. Alice's daughter
I wanted to hold his hand," the
all that he had meant to the girl

He came that evening to visit
visitors—Alice's sister and cousin
his hefty body at the other end o
comforter, and with weary grace
sugar in, more visitors came—th
apartment, who smoked cigar
for Alice and hers for them
sake, told of the ups and
curious relatives. But the
it was a family gatherin
the kitchen to rinse out
in a forlorn pitch.

Vera, the sister, piled h
and sat on a chair's arm, s
talks about living in a roon
with strangers, but it's only
If you've got nobody then it's
think so?" She strongly resembled
face, the tiny, almost skinny body—
she talked fast, she fidgeted. "I tol
The girls adore her, they think she
in another year if she wants to m
healthier thing to do then because

Joe looked down at his coffee cu
his large brown eyes that he was

"She doesn't know enough about
"God knows she's been through en
learn from your experiences, you
interesting living among strangers,
pretty soon she'll take up with som
think he knows all the answers b
know how to blow his own nose,"

The cousin returned from the ki
her big alligator purse over her t
Ruth, kissing her on the mouth, sa

The carpet in the hallway silenc
That sudden silence always aroused
a few minutes listening to what was
an anxious ear against the door, as
invitation? In that carpeted after
about Vera's lack of sisterly love, r

28

funeral of his dear friend
es in black, climbing into
d with a definite sense of
But when, on the long drive
ulously, "Where was Joe?
n her glimpsed reluctantly

ood Evening to the other
women—somberly settled
th who was lying under a
While he was stirring his
ired women from the next
alling their maternal love
nge the subject for Ruth's
ress shop to the shrewdly
on enough, realizing that
nent the cousin went into
tap water ran on and on

ver her black jersey dress
nd chatting with Joe. "She
it's good experience living
a family to come home to.
ate and you know it. You
arly hair, the large square
were of a different nature:
live with Gordon and me.
g seventeen and all. Then
ouse, that's fine. It'll be a
, she'll have us."

, saying appealingly with
give an opinion now.

p to her," Vera protested,
but at her age you don't
e'll think it's tragic and
'll belong to nobody and
a and papa to her. She'll
iot, when he won't even

furs, threw the strap of
The two women bent to

they left the apartment.
on that visitors stood for
m. Was Aunt Vera laying
actually would accept the
her mother's complaints
Continued on page 155)

e would go regularly to auction sales, and would buy old silver, old furniture, old carpets—anything that seemed to him to be going more cheaply than it should. His eye was good, and he rarely went wrong. If he had had some capital and more application he might have been a successful dealer: as it was, he was hardly more than a tout. He would take the bits he had bought back to his flat in South Kensington, and would sell them, at a profit, to his friends, or to friends of his friends.

But really there wasn't much of a living in it; and he would often have been in difficulty if it had not been for the young woman whom he referred to as his "girl friend," though she, like himself, was just over thirty years old. It was not that Noreen actually gave him money: he wouldn't have taken it, or at any rate he said he wouldn't have taken it. She sustained him even more directly. She fed him. She was the part-owner of a mock-rustic coffee-bar and light luncheon place, also in South Kensington; and Cullinan, the dealer, ate there regularly, for nothing, partaking day in and day out of the omelets, minestrones and cold ham salads that constituted the most substantial items of fare.

Noreen was well-to-do; she had a motorcar, and a little boy in boarding school—the child by her husband, from whom she had long been divorced. And Noreen was more assiduous than any other of Cullinan's friends in bringing prospective customers to the flat. Sometimes she would even pick them up in the café; for she, and the woman who owned the place with her, were in the habit of sitting and drinking coffee with their customers, that being part of the Bohemian, unbusinesslike charm of the place. Not that Noreen didn't have a sharp eye for a half crown: she did, indeed. The more was the pity then, her partner said more than once, that Noreen had let herself be taken in by a dud like Cullinan.

But Cullinan had a way with him. Between bites at his omelet he would reach out and, in full view of her customers, stroke Noreen's leg, or her hip. Or he would ignore her right through a meal, and then suddenly, as she bent over to take his last order for coffee, he would cover one hand of hers with his, silently, before saying, "Coffee, yes," and taking his hand away, so that the message between them would be secret, unspoken and, with the casualness of his order, brutal too. Publicly brutal or privately brutal, he had a way with him and it was always brutal.

In appearance, however, he was strained and fastidious enough, his shoulders slightly stooped, his hair rather long but very neat, his suit gray and City-ish, his blue eyes set closely together, with the skin across the high nasal bone drawn tight. Noreen should have known better, her partner said; and Noreen seemed to feel that she should have known better, for she had tried twice already to break away from him, but had failed both times. She had gone back to him, and offered him again her sturdy self to take. She loved him, she said—for look what she put up with from him!

It was with a view to helping Cullinan that Noreen talked at such length to the Australian, Sturgess. There were always colonials coming in and out of the coffee-bar—it was the sort of place to which they gravitated, from the boarding houses and hotels nearby. This one Noreen had seen several times before, and though she had not spoken to him she knew him for (Continued on page 149)

LOVE   PEACE   PARAPHERNALIA

29

The fresh-cut fragrance of East Indian Grass   carven's vétiver

30

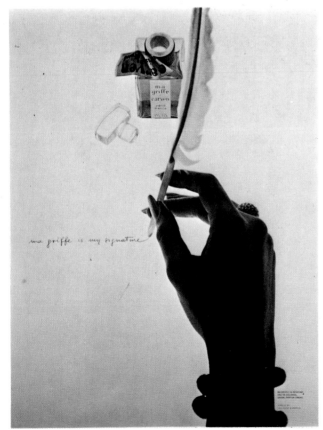

ma griffe is my signature

31

HOLIDAY

NOVEMBER 1968   75c

HOLIDAY

APRIL 1968   75c

OASIS TOUR OF
TUNISIA

JAMES A. MICHENER
ON SPAIN

IT'S A BIRD!
IT'S A PLANE!
NO—IT'S
SUPERPLANE!

SCOTLAND YARD'S
MYSTERY MUSEUM

HIPPIE MECCA
IN ISTANBUL

33

SHOW

THE
MAGAZINE
OF
THE
ARTS

75 CENTS
AUGUST 1962

MIDSUMMER SPECIAL:
Lolita's Private Life   Maugham's Memoirs   Lehar's Vienna   Ian Fleming's Workbook

34

SHOW

THE
MAGAZINE
OF
THE
PERFORMING
ARTS
$1.00
OCTOBER 1961

George Balanchine's world is bounded by

36

THE GREAT
CRAFTSMEN

MARANELLO, ITALY: FERRARI
In its years of production, the Ferrari has become the total triumph of the performance automobile in the world. Enzo Ferrari, now 65, an ex-racing driver, produces 600 of them a year. They are made by hand, each part being lovingly fashioned from the raw steel. Ferrari races his cars to a matter of pride—and to test their design. In a brief decade and a half, they have won more automobiles than any other make in all the history of the automobile.

The creation
of unique,
expensive,
handmade and
beautiful objects
survives,
brilliantly,
if precariously,
in odd corners
of Europe.
The pride and
love involved in
their making is
prodigious, and
their fame is
out of all
proportion to
their total number.
Photographs
and Text
by Henry Wolf

37

38

SHOW

39

SHOW

THE
MAGAZINE
OF
THE
ARTS

75 CENTS
MAY 1962

The two faces of Europe (and what's behind them)

40

SHOW

THE
MAGAZINE
OF
THE
PERFORMING
ARTS

$1.00
NOVEMBER 1961

41

paraphernalia New York, Los Angeles, Chicago, Davison, Paxon Co., Atlanta, Jordan Marsh, Miami, Kaufman's, Pittsburgh, May Co., Cleve., Wanamaker's, Phila.

42

Any Palizzio is better than no Palizzio

SHOES & HANDBAGS

43

HOW DO YOU MARRY A SCUBA DIVER?

NORMALLY, IN A HOUSE OF BIANCHI WEDDING DRESS.

44

DREAMS BEGIN WITH DANSKIN

There's still a long way to leap before the New York City Ballet asks for her hand. But even in her first Danskins she knew she was a prima ballerina. Danskin begins with the ambition and stays with it right up to center stage. Danskin tights, leotards, trunks, are full-fashioned knit of finest stretch nylon. Danskin at fine stores, dance supply houses or write us for catalogue D A. 437 Fifth Avenue, New York 10016. Division of Triumph Hosiery Mills. DANSKIN, INC.

45

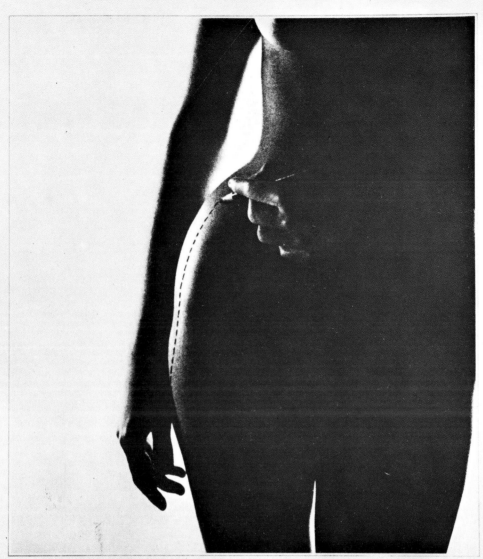

Wishful thinning?

Enhance by Lily of France

Cet ouvrage a été achevé
d'imprimer en mars 1971
par Bijutsu Shuppan-sha,
Tokyo. La photocompo-
sition a été confiée à l'Imprimerie Paul Attinger S.A.,
Neuchâtel (Suisse).
La maquette a été réalisée
par Gan Hosoya.

Imprimé et relié au Japon

This book was printed by
Bijutsu Shuppan-sha,
Tokyo. Photocomposition
by Imprimerie Paul Attinger,
S. A., Neuchâtel (Switzer-
land).
The lay-out was designed
by Gan Hosoya.

Printed and bound in Japan

Satz: Imprimerie
Paul Attinger S.A., Neu-
châtel (Schweiz).
Druck: Bijutsu Shuppan-
sha, Tokio.
Gestaltung: Gan Hosoya.

Printed and bound in Japan